Understanding Crypto

A Blockchain and Cryptocurrency Guide

Daniel Cawrey

Copyright © [2023] by [Daniel Cawrey]

Developmental Editor: Brett Noyes

Editor: Lynn Bodnar

Copyeditor: Carol Bush

Cover Design: Chelsea Jewell

Cover Concept: Brett Noyes

ASIN: B0BT8ZSRKY

Issued in the United States of America

Prologue

My name is Daniel Cawrey.

In 2011, I first read about Bitcoin in a magazine. I thought it sounded pretty silly even for someone with a computer science background working in the technology field. Digital money made sense, but the mining part of Bitcoin seemed unnecessary.

I decided at the time to revisit Bitcoin if it ever hit $100. It was worth $12 when I read that magazine article.

In the spring of 2013, the price of bitcoin went over $100. That's when I really got interested. I holed up in a room reading about Bitcoin for days on end in an attempt to completely understand it. And around that time, the cryptocurrency news site CoinDesk launched, which I started writing for as a Contributing Editor.

What you are about to read in this book is true. Everything in this guide has happened, and everything I've learned along the way about crypto is in here. Thanks for picking up this book. It really means a lot to me you're reading my words, and hopefully you'll learn a few things along the way.

Welcome to Understanding Crypto.

This book is dedicated to all my family and friends. A project like this does not come into the world without love and support.

My Dad for his humor through the laborious process of writing a book.

Brett Noyes and Steve Densmore for putting up with my random messages and reading my writing.

My Aunt Caroline for her perspective and sincere desire to listen to my stories.

My Grandmother Phyllis - still going strong and a role model for how to live long and healthy.

My two sisters, Aimee and Liz, for humor and great adventures we've been through together.

My high school English teacher Sue Mitchell who got me focused on reading and writing.

Special Thanks: Jeff Flowers, Ian Dixon, Bailey Reutzel, Elliott Williams, Zack Gow, Kyle Manna, Gregory DiPrisco, Alex Rass, Shayan Eskandari, Simon de la Rouviere, Vignesh Sundaresan, Roneil Rumburg, Jon Biggs, Lawrence Lewittinn, Scott Robinson, Margo Beller, Brad Keoun, Neil Reiter, Stan Higgins, James Foley, Brian Mosoff and James Wei

Contents

Introduction

Not long ago, it seemed like non-fungible tokens - NFTs - were everywhere. Celebrities, musicians and wealthy people were talking about these little cartoon characters. Artists, whether they were visual, musical or even writing TV shows were getting involved in the NFT space. A lot of hype surrounded NFTs. Yet most people don't understand exactly what an NFT is.

But hey, why should that matter? Someone's favorite artist has probably done a "drop" - the term for releasing NFTs. It's a thing that is only digital, these NFTs - a piece of visual art, a .wav file of some music or even poetry. For many people, this makes little sense. Why pay for these digital goods? Shouldn't they just be free? What's the value of things if they only exist on the internet?

And despite the hype that people have seen or heard, despite the amount of money involved (yes, someone paid $69 million for an NFT), the NFT world is currently really small.

Data from the website Sound.xyz is a glaring example. Sound.xyz is a site where musicians can drop new music and sell NFTs. Snoop Dogg's NFTs were released on Sound.xyz. And because blockchain data is free and openly available, it is easy to see that only over 10,000 addresses have interacted with NFTs at this site.

That's pretty small. But then again, the cryptocurrency industry has been trying to act larger than it really is for a long time. Marketing and PR campaigns rule the crypto world in an attempt to onboard the next million or even billion people. Problem is, marketing only does so much. People need education.

That's what "Understanding Crypto" was written for - an educational tool. This book dives right into what people need to know in the first chapter. Then, it journeys through the landscape of the cryptocurrency ecosystem today. There's a lot of hype in the blockchain world - and not enough education.

The truth is, cryptocurrency and blockchain are game-changing technologies. It's just still extremely early. Consider: Someone picking up this book and reading it today is still an early crypto adopter. Because someday, this technology is going to be used by billions. It's just not there yet. More smart thinkers need to enter the space, to help make cryptocurrency and blockchain usable for the masses.

There are a lot of criticisms about cryptocurrency and blockchain, and those are fair. Every new technology goes through a lot of skepticism before becoming mainstream. New ideas are often hard for many to wrap their heads around - until it becomes a thing everyone depends on. Automobiles. Television. Computers. Smartphones. All were dismissed, at first.

Crypto is just another one of those things. Eventually crypto will be something everyone uses, everyone depends on - oftentimes without even realizing it.

Why is there a spaceman on the cover? Because crypto advocates believe in the power of the technology so much, they often use the phrase "to the moon" to refer to its increases in price and in the potential it offers to reshape the ways we all think about money.

Quick Definitions Guide

Blockchain:

Blockchain is a system that securely records and verifies transactions across a network of computers, providing transparency and immutability.

Crypto:

Crypto, short for cryptocurrency, refers to digital or virtual currencies that use cryptography for secure financial transactions, control the creation of new units and verify the transfer of assets.

Cryptography:

Cryptography is the practice of using codes and algorithms to secure and protect information from unauthorized access or modification.

Cryptocurrency:

Cryptocurrency is digital money that uses cryptographic technology to secure transactions and control the creation of new units.

Hashing:

Hashing is a process of converting data into a fixed-size, unique string of characters, called a hash, using a mathematical algorithm.

Keys:

Keys are codes or data used to encrypt and decrypt information or to secure and access digital assets. They typically include a public key for encryption or sharing, and a private key for decryption or authorization.

Smart contracts:

Smart contracts are self-executing with the terms of an agreement directly written into software code. They automatically execute predefined actions and transactions when specific conditions are met, providing a decentralized and automated approach to enforce agreements without the need for intermediaries.

Gas:

Gas in the Ethereum payment system refers to the unit used to measure and allocate computational resources required to execute transactions or smart contracts on the Ethereum network.

Node:

A node refers to a computer or device that participates in the network by maintaining a copy of the blockchain and contributing to the validation and propagation of transactions. Nodes can be individuals, organizations or entities that help secure and maintain the blockchain network.

dapp (decentralized applications):

DApps, short for decentralized applications, are software applications that operate on a decentralized network, such as a blockchain, rather than relying on a centralized authority.

DeFi (decentralized finance):

DeFi refers to a financial system built on blockchain technology that aims to provide open and accessible financial services without the need for traditional intermediaries such as banks.

Open source:

Open source refers to a type of software or project that provides the source code to the public, allowing anyone to view, modify and distribute it freely.

Proof-of-stake:

Proof-of-stake (PoS) is a consensus algorithm used in blockchain networks. The probability of validating and receiving rewards is determined by the amount of crypto a participant holds and "stakes" in the network, rather than relying on computational power (as in proof-of-work).

Proof-of-work:

Proof-of-work (PoW) is a consensus algorithm used in blockchain networks, where participants solve complex computational puzzles to validate and add new blocks to the blockchain, requiring proven work via computational power as a measure of security.

Chapter One

Cryptography - The Foundation of Crypto

A lot of people already know about Bitcoin, the world's oldest cryptocurrency. In its earliest days, Bitcoin was considered a fad and a scam - and sometimes both. Today, its market capitalization, which is its price multiplied by the number of coins in circulation, is in the billions of dollars. But what many don't know is that cryptography - which has been around for thousands of years - is the backbone of Bitcoin and all other cryptocurrencies.

Cryptography Origins

To understand Bitcoin and cryptocurrency it's important to get to know cryptography, a foundational technology that makes it all work so well. Originated thousands of years ago to send communication during warring times, cryptography helps to secure bitcoin and other cryptocurrencies.

Cryptography has been around for thousands of years. From the era of the Romans to the internet's explosion in the 1990s, cryptography has been running the show in the background. And without it, there would certainly be no cryptocurrency!

The study of secure communications techniques cryptography comes from a Greek word, "kryptos", which means hidden. The first evidence of cryptography use comes from Egypt around 1900 B.C. Ancient Egyptians used pictorial writing, called hieroglyphics, to record their history and culture. Some of these cryptographic messages have not been completely deciphered to this day.

Ciphertext and the Romans

During the Roman Empire from 27 BC–476 AD, cryptography began to proliferate. Historians have long identified Julius Caesar as a risk-taker - he could have been a great entrepreneur. Julius Caesar was a pioneer in communications security and established the minting of coins for currency. He was the first Roman ruler to have an image of himself on a coin!

Caesar also pioneered ciphertexts, which are scrambled messages. Only readers that knew the code could decipher these messages. In Caesar's case, he would replace one letter with a different letter. The recipient would know a fixed number, go down the alphabet that number of positions and determine what letter was intended in the message and, presto, instant cipher!

Ciphertext was a useful form of secret communication for Caesar in Roman times and remained a prominent form of military communication until modern times. Modern ciphertext is exponentially more complex to create and decipher.

A similar form of ciphertext called Atbash was created during this time for the Hebrew language. In Atbash, the first letter of the alphabet becomes last, second becomes the second to last and so on. While effective in its time, these forms of ciphertext can be very quickly deciphered with today's technology.

Cryptanalysis

Increased use of cryptography in the Roman era led to increased demand to decipher it. The ability to decipher the enemy's code provided a gigantic strategic advantage that was obvious to many. That's where cryptanalysis comes in the picture.

Cryptanalysis is the art of deciphering encrypted messages. It was first documented in the Arab world. Linguist Al-Khalil ibn Ahmad al-Farahidi wrote about it in the "Book of Cryptographic Messages," around 750 AD - the first linguistic take on cryptography and cryptanalysis. The book is considered a foundational work for statistics, cryptocurrency and blockchain.

This work later inspired the creation of frequency analysis. Frequency analysis involves looking for patterns in communications. Discovering patterns allows a cipher to decode ciphertext, using the information to create what's known as a key. The "Book of Cryptographic Messages" was the first to list words with and without vowels in order for readers to study combinations.

Frequency analysis was one of many ways of deciphering enemy code. Another method was espionage, the practice of spying to get political and military information. The concept of key security arose in the 1880s - this is a concept important to cryptocurrency. Key security emerged as a way to protect written codes instead of relying on people to do so, which was problematic with the rise of espionage where people could flip from one side or another.

Cryptography in World Wars

The world of cryptanalysis became less of a linguistic practice in the 20th century and transitioned to a mathematical one, which is far more complex. Advancement of machines and early computers progressed the capability of cryptography. The world wars of the early 1900s were also a catalyst for advancement. The most well-known technology during this time was Germany's Enigma machine during World War II. It was capable of providing new keys every day, making it extremely difficult to decipher.

Global wars made adversaries wary of protecting communications. This left linguistic and lexicographic methods in the dust. The switch from simple text to more complicated data changed this. Militaries now could send and receive coordinates and complex instructions. As a result, specialized mathematicians known as cryptanalysts emerged during this time, with Britain's Alan Turing being the most famous of them all.

During World War II, the Germans had the initial advantage by creating new keys daily. In secret, British codebreakers built Colossus—the first programmable computer to break German ciphers. The most critical element of Colossus was its secrecy. The Germans continued to send critical information not knowing the enemy could read and react to these messages. Breaking the German ciphers led to the end of World War II, and the beginning of the Cold War.

Cryptanalysis is a form of engineering, but it is the first form of engineering that has a built-in enemy. This is because cryptanalysis and ciphers work in opposition. The opposition, the enemy, actually serves to make the cryptography stronger. Modern ciphers have been able to stay ahead of cryptanalysts since the world wars. But it is always a cat-and-mouse game.

In the information age, cryptographical communications is all the more a valuable asset.

To reiterate, a coded message is called an encrypted message. A decoded message is a deciphered or decrypted message. This is where the term encryption comes from. The properties of a modern cipher are twofold: They are both effective and fast. And the resources used to create it must be magnitudes larger than what it may take to break it.

Cold War Era

Before the 1970's, much of the research involving cryptography remained secret. This was due to the value cryptographic technology had to governments. Cryptography was a matter of national security as governments needed to keep communications and data out of the hands of adversaries. The Cold War was a period of informational, rather than physical, warfare.

In the early 1970's, IBM started conducting academic research on cryptography. As a result of this work, the U.S. Data Encryption Standard (DES) was developed. By this point, two major key standards developed, both with their own applications.

The first is called symmetric-key cryptography. In this application, both the sender and receiver receive the key. The second is public-key cryptography. This is where one key, the public one, is like a username. The second key, the private one, is like a password. Public-key cryptography is now widely used in cryptocurrency decades later.

Keys and Ciphers

During the Cold War era, two predominant encryption methods arose. The first was block ciphers, which allowed users to input plaintext (regular text) into blocks. The result is ciphertext that uses a cryptographic key and algorithm. For example, the data encryption standard, or DES, uses block ciphers. This standard enabled the encryption of large amounts of data, enabling consumer-related products to introduce cryptographic features. Examples include ATMs, email and secure remote access.

Stream ciphers are the second method. The main difference is that stream ciphers convert plain text 1 byte ata time, so stream ciphers make it possible to use individual characters. This technology offers speed and would later be integrated into wireless internet technology.

The most important thing to remember is that cryptography works on a system of digital keys. Scrambling information doesn't do any good if there isn't a way to decode it. This was true in Caesar's times, and it is still true today. As technology became more complicated over time, so did the methods of coding and decoding. But still cryptography was all about symmetric key and public-key encryption.

Remember, symmetric key cryptography requires the use of one key. That single key both encrypts and decrypts. Think of a door with a lock on it. It has a key that locks and unlocks it. Whoever has access to this key can lock or enter the location.

Public key cryptography uses two keys. The first is a public-key used as an identifier, while the second is a private key kept hidden as a hardened, unchangeable password. Think of an email account that has a username and a password.

Internet Technology

Worldwide use of the web and email caused the proliferation of encryption in the mainstream, although most people didn't notice. This was particularly true for email as it first applied public-key cryptography for digital communications. Message confidentiality in the form of encryption was essential. This is, in essence, the digital version of Julius Caesar sending critical messages to his generals.

The early days of email predated public-key cryptography use. Early email actually utilized a symmetric key (one single key to unlock) design. However, symmetric cryptography uses a system that has its flaws. In this system, encrypted data and the key would be sent with the message. If the message could somehow be decoded, all system messages could be deciphered. This posed a security threat for all users of email.

Without the innovation of public-key cryptography, the internet might have lacked the privacy needed for things like email. But remember, the second key is private and should be treated with great care as it is the "password." And unlike email, be aware that changing this password or getting recovery if it's lost, in cryptocurrency, can be hard and almost impossible today.

In email communication, there are two primary parties. The first is the sender, and the second is the receiver. When an email is sent, the sender requests the recipient's public key. When a message arrives, the recipient is then able to decipher the message with the private key.

The user "signs" the two keys together in order to decipher and read the message. All of this happens in the background without the user's explicit knowledge. This is the basics of how encrypted email works. A similar system is used in cryptocurrencies!

Cypherpunks

By the 1990s, the use of email and the consumer internet was becoming mainstream. With that, concerns regarding user privacy started to arise with many technologists. Because of this, a group that called themselves cypherpunks, began to emerge. The cypherpunks considered themselves advocates for online privacy.

The founders of the cypherpunks consisted of Eric Hughes, Timothy C. May and John Gilmore. They were having regular meetings in the San Francisco Bay Area starting in 1992. The group started a mailing list that grew to 2,000 subscribers by 1997. A key figure participating in the cypherpunk movement also included David Chaum, a proponent of digital money.

Many governments in the 20th century considered cryptography to be a weapon and wanted to keep its technological innovations secret. Members of the cypherpunk movement were skeptical of governments, however, fearing more nefarious intentions. Cypherpunks believe that privacy is a human right. They have a healthy suspicion of the government and its motives. Cypherpunks believe, just like Julius Caesar, that technology, specifically the use of cryptography, can make things better for a technology-enabled society. The cypherpunks are considered by many a predecessor to cryptocurrency pioneers.

Cypherpunk founding member Eric Hughes wrote the seminal book, "A Cypherpunk's Manifesto" in 1993. Hughes coined the phrase, "Privacy is necessary for an open society in the electronic age". The cypherpunks' primary concern was that governments would withhold cryptography from society as a method of control. They believed that democratic countries should allow public use of cryptography.

The Cypherpunks may have seemed to be the alarmists of their time. In the 1990s, they foretold a world where personal privacy would become a huge concern. Those fears seem to have come to fruition. Today many organizations, from governments to multinational companies, are in possession of sensitive data. And time and time again, this information is breached. This information eventually becomes available to criminals for nefarious uses on the dark web. All of this was a major concern of the Cypherpunks back in the 90s, and it is a reality today.

Modern Encryption

In the early days of the internet, most data was stored in unencrypted databases. This included sensitive information, such as passwords. It's hard to imagine now, but user passwords were often stored in databases as plaintext. This means stored "plainly" so that anyone with access could see the information - as it says, plain text.

Nowadays, this would seem unthinkable.

Over time, data protection has grown into a huge industry. In 1978, a public key system was created by inventors Ron Rivest, Adi Shamir and Leonard Adleman - which is known today as RSA encryption. In 1982, RSA DATA Security was founded as the first data security company. Pretty Good Privacy, or PGP, which arrived in 1991, provided publicly-available tools for cryptography. These tools once had only been available to governments.

Standards such as RSA and PGP were not designed for the average user. Only tech-savvy people like the cypherpunks could use them. However, over time, these tools and security practices have become more widely available and easy to use. PGP tools are now available for any email user. The RSA annual conference is now the top internet security conference.

Early Digital Monies

Cryptography is the foundation of the modern web. Without it, online commerce would not have blossomed in the 1990s. So thank Julius Caesar for that free 2-day shipping one of these days. Because without proper encryption, users would not feel safe sharing payment information with e-commerce providers in the first place. All because of the Roman Empire! Who would have thought.

In the early days of what would become known as e-commerce, it wasn't always safe to use credit cards online. Early e-commerce providers did not have the tools to securely store customer data. This presented an opportunity for both criminals and entrepreneurs.

A new wave of bad actors referred to as cybercriminals emerged due to the opportunity to steal from web users. At the same time, online pioneers saw an opportunity to build a global online marketplace, and so companies like PayPal, Ebay and Amazon emerged. These companies brought in a new era of commerce.

The need for some kind of digital money was obvious to early internet pioneers. Today, there is an exchange of sensitive personal data for goods and services. The hope of digital currency is to make this exchange without giving away so much personal data.

Money was being digitized well before the internet became popular - back in the 1970s. Banks started issuing debit cards in 1978 for business executives with large expenses. Financial institutions could see change coming but were slow to move. Small upstart innovators had the advantage.

Digicash

In 1989, Digicash was the first effort in this vein founded by David Chaum. Digicash facilitated anonymous digital payments online years before people started using Amazon. Chaum had invented something called Blind Signature Technology (BST) at the University of California, Santa Barbara in 1983. BST uses cryptography to protect the privacy of payments online, utilizing encryption-based mathematics to obscure information. This was one of the earliest attempts to make secure payments online.

Digicash even had its own currency known as Cyberbucks. Yep, no joke, literally Cyberbucks. Users would sign up for the Digicash service and in return get some free Cyberbucks. Oftentimes, Cyberbucks would be referred to as tokens or coins, which is terminology now often used for various cryptocurrencies.

Digicash was an early adopter of microchipped smart cards. Decades later, this technology is used on almost all credit cards for security - it's that little bronze square embedded in the plastic. Digicash was also an early innovator in the concept of a digital wallet for storing value, in this case, the Cyberbucks. Not sure why they didn't call it a Cyberwallet for the Cyberbucks, but whatever. There were merchants during this time that signed up to accept Cyberbucks. Digicash even had Encyclopedia Britannica among its early customers. However, just like the fate of print encyclopedias, there were few customers who actually used the service.

Digicash was adopted by a few financial firms, including Deutsche Bank. During the 1990s, ecommerce was very new. People were pretty hesitant to use credit cards on the web. They were even more skeptical about using a new type of payment system that only existed on the internet. Many privacy-conscious users did, however, adopt Cyber-bucks. These users even developed a mailing-list marketplace for a period of time, but it never was able to achieve traction due to a lack of merchants. The Digicash company finally filed for bankruptcy in 1998.

E-Gold

Many think Bitcoin was the first digital store of value, but it was not. In 1996, E-Gold was its predecessor. It was a digital gold currency. This means digital gold units were backed by real units of gold—operated by a company called Gold & Silver Reserve. E-Gold enabled instant transfers between its users on the internet. Everything on the platform was denominated in units of gold or other precious metals.

The platform was the first to introduce micropayments on the internet. A micropayment is a small transaction, usually carried out online, that can be as small as a fraction of a cent. E-Gold was able to process denominations as small as 0.0001 gram of gold. Other innovations included an application programming interface (API) for software developers. This enabled the creation of other services on top of the E-Gold platform. Merchants accepted E-Gold as a form of payment alongside credit cards. E-Gold began offering support for mobile payments in 1999.

By 2006, there were over 3.5 million E-Gold accounts, and the company was processing more than $2 billion in yearly volume on a monetary base of $71 million in gold bullion. E-Gold made major technical contributions to online payments through the early 2000s. However, the system was plagued with problems from its onset, which eventually led to its demise.

One of E-gold's flaws was its centralization, because it compromised integrity and trustworthiness in the system. Which included, as a centralized entity, that platform did not have sufficient identity verification mechanisms, and so it was also used for nefarious purposes. It facilitated money laundering, online scams, and other illegal activity. The US government finally shut down E-Gold in 2008.

Hashcash

Invented by Adam Back in 1997, Hashcash introduced the idea of proof-of-work. Proof-of-work is a way to force computers to produce some kind of computation-intensive output; basically a way to verify something. HashCash used cryptography to enable this, and Back proposed using an algorithm called SHA1. The concept of proof-of-work is a cornerstone of Bitcoin and other cryptocurrencies. It will be discussed in greater detail in the following chapters.

Back proposed the idea of adding a "postage" fee to email to reduce spam using digital currency. By utilizing a "hash" that required computer processing in the form of proof-of-work, there was an economic cost, which would theoretically limit spam in email systems. This application of the technology never took off.

HashCash's proof-of-work hashing power innovation solved something called the "double-spend problem". Double-spending is when a digital unit is duplicated and spent more than once. It is basically the digital equivalent of counterfeiting cash. Computers make it easy to replicate files. Anyone can copy an image file and reproduce it over and over. But by using hashing, this makes it more costly and prohibitive to duplicate or double-spend something.

HashCash was tested in email systems, such as Microsoft. However, the concept of paying for little-to-no spam did not take off. HashCash as a concept would prove problematic in digital money systems. It increased computing power and caused the system to create monetary inflation and reduce value over time. This exposed the need to solve the problem of virtual scarcity - limiting the amount of digital currency in circulation. Bitcoin later accomplished this with the use of a fixed supply.

B-Money

B-Money, invented by Wei Dai in 1998, introduced the concept of creation of digital money. Particularly interesting is that this money would be created through computations - a money issued without government involvement. This was another early approach for the idea of proof-of-work cryptocurrency, which would arrive later.

In a sense, the theory with B-Money was that the cost of creating digital money would be calculated from the computer power used to create it. This digital money would be priced based on a basket of real-world assets. These assets could in theory include gold or other scarce commodities. And a limited supply would prevent this money from inflating or losing value over time.

B-Money also advanced the idea of broadcasting transactions to a network. The system would be enforceable via a system of digital contracts, which then would be used to resolve any disputes. Dispute resolution how credit card companies deal with problems like chargebacks, which is a term in the financial industry for when a transaction is reversed for fraud or other reasons. The B-Money system would use cryptography to enforce contractual issues, introducing the concept of smart contracts, an important tool for software development of cryptocurrencies (as discussed later with Ethereum).

B-Money brought together various components of digital cash. This almost sounds silly today but was a totally new concept in the 1990s. It applied the idea of contractual obligations to provide order to an anonymous and distributed system and this novel concept of using something called proof-of-work in the form of computer power to create money.

Bit Gold

B-Money was a theoretical exercise by its creator, Wei Dai. The purpose was to explore the concept of non-governmental money, or money that might not be subject to inflation via a controlled money supply. In 1998, Bit Gold was proposed by computer scientist Nick Szabo. Bit Gold proposed to bring the scarcity of real-world assets into the digital world. It was one of the earliest attempts at creating a decentralized digital currency.

Bit Gold built upon the core concepts of E-Gold by adding scarcity of assets. For example, gold is valuable because it is unique, scarce and takes considerable cost to mine. Szabo applied these concepts to digital assets. The design also used a puzzle type of proof-of-work. The system proposed a timestamped "challenge string" generated on a user's computer. This would then be submitted for proof of ownership.

Similar to B-Money, the Bit Gold project was never implemented. The theories proposed, however, had a substantial impact on future digital currencies. Because of this, many consider Bit Gold as one of the precursors to Satoshi Nakamoto's Bitcoin protocol. Since Nakamoto's identity is unknown, some speculate that Szabo could be him, but Szabo denies this.

PayPal

Online payments pioneer PayPal was founded in 1998. At the time, it was revolutionary for internet users because the company could process payments safer and more securely than credit cards. PayPal served as a trusted middleman between financial institutions and online stores. One of the ways it did this is by using encryption, PayPal could safely store sensitive customer credit card information.

A key component of PayPal's success was its integration with eBay, an online auction site. eBay customers were given a choice to use credit cards or PayPal. Another element of PayPal's ascendancy was that the company deployed a referral program, and new users received $10 for signing up. Once users joined up, they experienced a simple and secure check-out process, and were instantly hooked.

Behind the simple PayPal check-out process was a much more secure payment method, again, using encryption. This method reduced the security risk for the customer buying something online, the financial institution processing the payment and the merchant selling something on the web. And it was encryption creating this trust and security to create a better customer experience.

PayPal went public in 2002 and was quickly acquired by eBay. It was later spun off as a separate company in 2014. The company now has hundreds of millions of users. Today, Paypal accounts can even buy or sell many popular cryptocurrencies.

In the End

Cryptography is not a new concept. It is a technology that has been used throughout time to communicate and transfer value. It was Julius Caesar's way to secretly communicate with his generals - can you imagine what he would think now? And many of these ideas covered here would later converge - starting with the conceptualization and creation of the Bitcoin network.

Things to Know From This Chapter:

- Cryptography is not new - a form of it was relied upon by Julius Caesar in Roman and impacted modern world wars

- Cryptography (and cryptocurrency) works on a system of keys

- Internet technology started as shockingly unsecured without the use of cryptography, private info was easily obtained by all

- Security, protection, passwords, the "keys", have naturally grown very sophisticated

Chapter Two

Bitcoin

T he story of modern cryptocurrency starts in the dark corners of the internet.

In 2008, the global economy was experiencing a financial crisis. The greed of financial institutions was to blame. This economic situation would lead to what is now known as the Great Recession. In response to the state of the world, an anonymous source sent a nine-page whitepaper to a cryptography mailing list on October 31, 2008.

Whitepaper

This whitepaper, "Bitcoin: A Peer-to-Peer Electronic Cash System," entailed an alternative financial system. The paper laid the groundwork for modern cryptocurrencies. The first proponents consisted of a group of counterculture-type figures. Cypherpunks, libertarians, anarchists and eventually criminals were drawn to the concept of Bitcoin.

Sounds like a great premise of a Hollywood movie? Well, it definitely would be if more was known about its originators. The founding figures, those who actually wrote the Bitcoin whitepaper, remain shrouded to this day. The anonymous writer of the whitepaper went by the name Satoshi

Nakamoto and their true identity remains unknown. Mystery regarding the whitepaper's origins has helped to create a great mythology around Bitcoin.

The Bitcoin whitepaper set everything for cryptocurrencies into orbit. It envisioned a peer-to-peer, or person-to-person, electronic payment technology. Bitcoin sought to avoid traditional financial institutions within its system. It was an idea designed to theoretically distribute financial power back to the individual.

2008 Financial Crisis and Bitcoin

Many grew suspicious of banks in the 2000s. The Cypherpunks, for instance, were already critical of the powerful and inequitable financial system. The Bitcoin whitepaper aligned with many existing beliefs in the counterculture and provided a roadmap to create a new financial system. It basically proposed a digital currency for the internet. This was different from existing payment systems. Bitcoin would utilize cryptography as its trust system in place of financial institutions.

Transactions in this new system would be grouped into "blocks" that would be "hashed" into a permanent "chain". A hash function turns an input of information into a string of bytes with a fixed length and structure - something easily readable by computers.

This would be done using cryptography and a system of computers all over the world working together in a distributed fashion. Basically, a financial network that didn't need third-party verification like a bank to act as a middleman. Usually, transaction verification is done by banks, but this Bitcoin concept removed the need for any one institution or third party as the source of trust.

Crypto Transactions

Clearly, this proposed Bitcoin idea was quite contrary to established payment systems. In a traditional system, transactions are private. In the Bitcoin system, transactions are all visible on the network, on the blockchain, that "chain" of blocks of data. Participants in this system that process these blocks of data, are called "nodes." Nodes are basically computers on the network that verify transactions.

These nodes use cryptography to solve a small puzzle using a standard known as SHA-256. Solved puzzles would then be broadcasted to the network and verified by other nodes. Once verified, the collection of transactions or blocks of data would be published to the larger chain of information, called the blockchain. After publication, transactions cannot be changed, as all data on the blockchain is "immutable" or permanent.

This verification system would go on to become what is known as Bitcoin mining. And mining would be incentivized with transaction fees and the generation of new bitcoins. This is why many people were motivated and would want to be joined up to the network. Bitcoin would be created daily but on a sliding scale to slowly taper the total circulation. After all, limited circulation creates scarcity. The scarcity of a commodity in the real world often creates value, especially if supply is less than demand.

The Bitcoin whitepaper outlined that only 21 million BTC, an abbreviation for units of bitcoin, would ever be created. This provided a limited supply of the asset, giving it value - kind of like a digital version of gold. People who purchased bitcoin would eventually hold onto it instead of using it for payments. People that hold bitcoin regardless of its appreciation or depreciation are called "hodlers" (pronounced: HOHD-lers). They believe that the fixed supply will cause it to have significant value in the future.

Open source project

Satoshi Nakamoto was able to impress highly technical people with the Bitcoin whitepaper. One such person was Hal Finney, a software developer who was one of the first programmers to work on Pretty Good Privacy (PGP), a cryptography-based communication tool. Finney had worked with cryptography pioneer and PGP Corporation founder Phil Zimmerman.

A self-proclaimed Cypherpunk, Finney was a big fan of David Chaum's Digicash. He believed there was a massive reduction in personal privacy with the progression of technology. He had long believed internet-enabled personal computers could be tools for liberation and freedom. Finney was the first person to receive a bitcoin transaction from Satoshi Nakamoto once the network went live. He famously wrote on Twitter on January 10, 2009 he was "Running bitcoin". Finney passed away in 2014 and is considered a legendary figure in the crypto world.

Another early proponent of Satoshi's work was Gavin Andresen. A computer scientist, Andresen discovered the Bitcoin concept shortly after the publication of the whitepaper. Andresen created the first bitcoin faucet, a precursor to what is now generally known as an airdrop. Airdrops are the distribution of small amounts of cryptocurrency, used as an incentive to increase overall crypto adoption.

Both Finney and Andresen were regular communicators with Satoshi Nakamoto. No one is sure of Nakamoto's gender or whether they are one person or a group. An analysis of Satoshi's writing and times of day of writing has suggested the author lived in Europe. As of this writing, Satoshi Nakamoto controls over 1 million bitcoin mined in the early days.

Bitcoin Foundations

The first bitcoin blockchain address is:

1A1zP1eP5QGefi2DMPTfTL5SLmv7DivfNa.

The transparent nature of the blockchain allows anyone to verify this. It can be looked up using something called a block explorer, an essential blockchain tool that takes blockchain data and posts it on the web.

That address is one of the thousands of Satoshi Nakamoto's bitcoin addresses. The Genesis Block, which is the name for the first block on the Bitcoin chain, has a peculiarity to it. The original 50 BTC that was sent cannot be spent because of how Bitcoin's software - often simply referred to as "Core" for its full name "Bitcoin Core" - was designed.

"BTC" is often used to denote bitcoin in markets like a stock ticker. "XBT" is also used as a symbol for bitcoin. The currency is known as "bitcoin," in lowercase, while the uppercase "Bitcoin" refers to the network. This is according to CoinDesk's official style guide. CoinDesk is the largest information resource about the crypto and blockchain industry.

Remember, Bitcoin public keys are like a username - albeit a username that is very long and very difficult to remember. Public keys are randomly generated strings of numbers and letters. There's nothing special to it; public keys are simply random.

Bitcoin uses the Elliptic Curve Digital Signature Algorithm, or ECDSA. To get a bit technical, it uses something called secp256k1 to generate the keys. First, the private key is created using ECDSA. Then, subsequently, the public key is made. Private and public keys are randomly generated, secure, and immutable. While this sounds complex, the important concept here is that their use is not a lot more complicated than a username and password system.

Mining

The innovative design of mining allows the Bitcoin network to remain secure. This is done without the miners actually needing to know anything about users on the Bitcoin network. And that's all backed - secured - by cryptography.

Bitcoin miners (those who verify transactions in nodes) use a special algorithm called SHA-256. SHA stands for Secure Hash Algorithm, and 256 represents the number of bits used. A bit is the smallest unit of data that can be processed and stored. For example, whatever input is used, the output will be 256 bits. This provides some flexibility. One bit is the smallest amount of information in computing, and 256 bits is enough to provide data detailing each transaction without clogging the network. SHA-256 is not new, and there are other variations of it, depending on bit length.

So, how does this SHA-256 algorithm actually work to secure Bitcoin? It uses something called "hashing". Hashing takes information, such as a password, and scrambles it so it can remain private and secure. It's important to know that this SHA algorithm isn't only used for bitcoin. Password encryption, digital signatures and Secure Socket Layer, or SSL, provide critical technology that is used for lots of digital security applications.

Transactions

The Bitcoin network is an evolution. It is a digital financial system that needs all the tools of a real-world system for moving value, like traditional payment networks such as Visa or PayPal. These new crypto tools are being built in real time as new users enter the system. One such tool is a wallet, something akin to an account for storing bitcoin.

Bitcoin uses something called UTXO, or Unspent Transaction Output, to process transactions. The system is similar to a physical cash system, with inputs and outputs. It is important to see the lifecycle of a bitcoin to better understand how this works. As an example, 1 BTC is created through a mining process known as a coinbase transaction. This brand new bitcoin has no inputs and one or more outputs. This is the new bitcoin for this transaction example.

Now, let's say this miner wants to spend 0.5 BTC. The Bitcoin network uses one input to send that amount, but since the previous output was 1 BTC and not 0.5, an input is created for that 0.5 amount. The difference in value is returned. Sounds confusing? Think about bitcoin's UTXO model as spending cash. An item costs $0.50. The person buying hands the cashier $1.00. In return, the person buying receives the difference of $.50.

This is a simplified way of understanding the UTXO model. Bitcoin improved on design flaws of previous digital currencies by this UTXO model combined with a blockchain. The technology allows all inputs and outputs to be auditable and secure. And this can be done without the use of any third-party verification.

Double Spending

It is important to understand how transactions work on the Bitcoin network, because it is different from payments using digital networks such as credit and debit cards. With regular payments, one person sends money to a recipient. The sender has money debited, and the recipient's account is credited. This is a very basic way to explain how most payments work, and this commonly understood simplification helps to understand how a bitcoin payment operates differently.

The 'double-spend problem' is an issue that plagued early digital currencies prior to the advent of Bitcoin. It is just really easy to duplicate and distribute digital files. For example, digital images and music files are easily copied and transferred. In the same way, it has been hard to create a digital currency that would not have this same problem - until cryptography was used.

The accounting model of UXTO helps to solve this issue. Like physical cash, the UXTO model makes a bitcoin, or even a fraction of it, very hard to spend more than once.

Bitcoin's design makes it easy to generate new addresses. This stands in contrast to traditional financial systems. In the traditional financial system, account creation is slow or cumbersome. However, in the case of cryptocurrencies, one person or entity could control many addresses. This is because, in the UTXO model, addresses are not imprinted on the blockchain itself. Rather, transaction outputs use a reference to an address known as scriptPubKey.

Hosted Wallets

Many cryptocurrency services use "hosted wallets" to take care of everything for customers. It makes for a much more seamless customer experience for cryptocurrency users. A centralized exchange, for example, refers to the use of software owned by a company to help conduct transactions that have hosted wallets. For example, Coinbase and Bitstamp are two of many centralized cryptocurrency exchanges. They serve as trusted parties to facilitate transactions and hold user funds.

These services hold users' private keys, which is done for user security and safety. Many new crypto users are not familiar with the cryptography key system and consider cryptocurrency wallets like bank accounts. This is why many cryptocurrency services take care of the private key for users.

It's important to remember the phrase: "Not your keys, not your coins". If a user does not have direct possession of the crypto keys, there isn't full control over the cryptocurrency. For this reason, it is important to use a trusted cryptocurrency exchange service. Many hacks and thefts have occurred because a service was not secure.

A crypto wallet is like an account. But in the background, there is a system of cryptography and keys. While each exchange and wallet deploys a proprietary key storage system, no two services are alike. Investing in cryptocurrency may start as a hobby. Over time, many people may accumulate a significant amount of value. This is why it is important to do research on which exchanges and wallets to use.

Software Forks

Since Bitcoin is an open-source project, it is free and available for anyone to use. Many people have been able to take the software and use it to create other cryptocurrencies. This is called a "software fork." This is where the software code delves onto another path, like a fork in the road.

There are several types of forks when it comes to crypto: Software forks, soft forks and hard forks. Software forks in the crypto world have been common, especially utilizing Bitcoin's code. The best-known software fork of Bitcoin is called Litecoin.

Charlie Lee is Litecoin's founder, a former Google engineer with an early interest in cryptocurrency. Lee took Bitcoin's software and changed some of the parameters. He then launched his own cryptocurrency, Litecoin, which will be discussed further in the Other Cryptocurrencies chapter.

Soft Forks

A "soft fork" is different from a software fork, as it is a blockchain-based fork. This means that it is a change to a live cryptocurrency network and the rules that define it. Soft forks are used to upgrade blockchains. Unlike other software, with crypto there is a permanent ledger, the blockchain, that provides an immutable or unchangeable trail of information. That's why a crypto community - like the one that supports Bitcoin - cannot simply update the software at will.

With a soft fork, what to do with transaction history and how to maintain its integrity has to be carefully considered first before making any changes. Forks also require the majority of proof-of-work miners (that large network of verifiers) to upgrade their software in order for it to be effective.

Those who do not upgrade during a forking event may begin to see rejected transactions on the network as their software is no longer compatible.

A soft fork usually adds features or updates the security of a blockchain and must be backward compatible with previous transactions. This means that the copy must be a replica of the original, as original transactions are immutable because of the miner's previous verifications.

Hard Forks

A "hard fork", on the other hand, is a major change to the protocol. This is different in that this type of fork can invalidate transactions. Again, like a soft fork, miners must signal their willingness to upgrade their software for a hard fork. A hard fork is a very drastic measure to take with a blockchain. It's usually due to a security issue or some reaction to the workings of an existing cryptocurrency network. It requires significant effort to do, as it requires complete miner approval (perhaps like getting every single dog owner in your neighborhood to pick up after their pooch). And unlike soft forks which can make small changes, miners aren't always incentivized to want huge changes to a cryptocurrency.

Hard forks can have serious consequences. It also shows how important the mechanism of consensus is in the Bitcoin network. The ability to out-pace a blockchain creates a vulnerability for a double-spend opportunity. An early hard fork in 2010 for Bitcoin, for example, showed that forks could leave the network vulnerable to a double-spend attack. During the split, a person was able to make a transaction more than once. Luckily, this action was done only to test the system's vulnerabilities.

Many organized bitcoin hard forks have been proposed. For instance, BitcoinXT was launched by early bitcoin developer Mike Hearn. It was designed to run transactions faster and increased the average number of transactions per second from seven to 24. This hard fork increased the size of Bitcoin blocks from 1 megabyte to 8 megabytes of storage space.

Hard forks need all the miners to agree to an upgrade. With BitcoinXT, Hearn was not able to garner enough support, and Hearn left the Bitcoin community in 2015 to pursue other blockchain projects. Yet Hearn's project exposed a major flaw with the Bitcoin network: Transaction speeds. How could Bitcoin's "peer-to-peer" payment system be possible with only seven transactions per second? (Consider Visa makes 1,700 transactions per second and up to 24,000 during peak times). That speed is very slow compared to the traditional payment system and actually became an obstacle to user adoption.

The Bitcoin Community's Ideological Split

Bitcoin is not controlled by a single person or corporation. It is a community-led, open source software project. While this is great in theory, the community is not always in agreement as to how cryptocurrencies should develop and progress. This has led to some community leaders leaving to start alternative blockchains.

It's important at this point to discuss the motivation and ideology that created Bitcoin. Satoshi Nakamoto's own actions provide some insight. The Genesis block, the very first Bitcoin block ever mined, contains this text:

The Times 03/Jan/2009 Chancellor on brink of second bailout for banks

This references a London Times front-page article on that date. It suggests that bitcoin was invented because of or as a response to the 2008 financial crisis.

The Libertarian ideology believes that markets should trade without regulation or government oversight. Many Libertarians became first adopters of Bitcoin with an interest in it being used as an alternative payment system. While Libertarians used Bitcoin early on for ideological reasons, another group used it for nefarious reasons.

In the early days of Bitcoin, many people thought its transactions could not be tracked. Between 2011 and 2013, a "dark web market" called Silk Road emerged. A dark web market allows its users to buy and sell illegal items anonymously on these platforms and bitcoin was the payment method on Silk Road. Many tended to consider Bitcoin anonymous because of features like the UTXO model. However, Bitcoin is actually considered pseudonymous as data science can be used to make a lot of conclusions about the movement of funds.

Blockchain analysis firms are able to collect data like addresses from exchanges and wallets to track the movement of bitcoin. The Bitcoin system provides increased privacy - but only those who know how to use it properly. Many would learn later on that all transactions on the blockchain can be tracked. Circumstantial conclusions can be made about who made these transactions. Privacy cryptocurrencies, such as Monero, would focus on anonymity, but most cryptocurrencies are pretty trackable.

The goal of the Bitcoin network is to create a decentralized monetary system. Both flaws and strengths of the system continue to be exposed, and some have believed that these flaws cannot be fixed within the current Bitcoin system. This had led to the Bitcoin community splitting, eventually causing a fork.

Is Bitcoin a Payment or Store of Value System?

Credit cards across the major networks of Visa, Discover and Amex can process 5,000 payments a second. In 2022, the total volume for credit card networks was over $9 trillion. The scale of consumer payments is immense—and fast. Bitcoin as a payment network is small, and unfortunately, it is currently pretty slow.

Bitcoin transactions need block confirmations - it's part of the network's design and security. Because of this, the average Bitcoin block confirmation time can take up to 10 minutes. Those considering using bitcoin as money on the internet, as a quick payment method, wanted to figure out a way to make the network faster.

Hashcash's Adam Back, who later became a figure in the cryptocurrency world, believed future technologies would increase Bitcoin's overall speed. Back and others championed the idea of "Layer 2" technology for Bitcoin. Built on top of the existing software, Layer 2 would also help to speed up transactions.

Bitcoin Layer 2

An example of Layer 2 software for Bitcoin is something called Lightning Network. With this design, which has been worked on for many years, Bitcoin would act as a "settlement layer". Then the Lightning Network would be used as the Layer 2 technology to interact. Users would interface with Lightning Network to pay for things using bitcoin. This would, in essence, be its own payments accounting mechanism using the blockchain to then reconcile payments.

To move in this direction, a hard fork called Segregated Witness, or SegWit, was proposed by Bitcoin Core developer Peter Wuille. A Bitcoin Core developer is someone who is a maintainer of the Bitcoin software codebase and their input has great merit. The idea of SegWit was to change the way data was stored on the blockchain without changing block speeds and block times. It would offer more flexibility to Bitcoin going forward. Segregated Witness was implemented in August 2017.

Another group at this time proposed Bitcoin Cash, which allowed 8-megabyte blocks every ten minutes. After much contention with miners, Bitcoin Cash was also launched in August 2017. As a result of Bitcoin Cash, a group of miners began rejecting Bitcoin blocks, causing a hard fork. This created two different chains. Owners of bitcoin were able to redeem the same amount of bitcoin cash from that network, using the past chain to verify ownership.

There are other bitcoin hard forks, such as Bitcoin Gold and Bitcoin SV. These forks have different ideas about the future of bitcoin. None of these competing chains are nearly as popular as the original, however. Many have branched off to create a more efficient payment system. To date, none of them have succeeded yet.

Maturation of Bitcoin Mining

When it comes to security issues, the Bitcoin community has in the past banded together to fix flaws in the software's code. This was done in 2013. A block with more transactions than miners could handle was sent to the network. The community identified the issue and solved it. This was accomplished by reverting back to an earlier version of the software.

One of the reasons why this happened was because, at that time, bitcoin mining was a hobbyist activity. It was something done on personal computers. Today, anyone can download the bitcoin software, Bitcoin Core, and run a node. However, regular computers are no longer able to compete in the mining race to validate new transactions or mine new bitcoin. This is because competition has become very high as the price of bitcoin has increased. Commercial miners now use very specialized machines, rendering the hobbyist miner obsolete.

Large companies, some of them publicly traded on stock markets, are now the leaders in cryptocurrency mining. These companies utilize specialized equipment, known as application specific instruction chips, or ASICs, to solve the computational problems to validate transactions on the Bitcoin blockchain. This equipment is housed in data centers spanning tens or hundreds of thousands of square feet. In addition, these companies also offer hosting services to clients, allowing customers to share in the cost of a data center. All of this has pretty much rendered the hobbyist Bitcoin miner obsolete - although there are some other smaller cryptocurrencies where this is still possible.

Bitcoin Mining and China

Initially, as ASICs took over, China emerged as the global leader in Bitcoin mining. However, China has been an unstable environment for Bitcoin and crypto mining. The Chinese seem to view Bitcoin as a threat to both its central bank and government.

In spite of this, 70% of the world's Bitcoin has been mined in mainland China. The concentration of mining has often created significant volatility and risk for the industry. Case in point: As China set its goal to reach carbon neutrality by 2060, it has banned crypto mining companies.

As a result, cryptocurrency miners moved to Kazakhstan and Russia due to their proximity. They also relocated operations to places like the U.S., Canada or Ireland for a more stable political climate. The U.S. now accounts for a good amount of the global hashrate. Miners also naturally gravitate to locations that offer sustainable, renewable and cheaper energy sources. Kazakhstan, Russia, Canada and Ireland make up the top five in miner share globally.

Lending Market

In addition to derivatives, a market for bitcoin borrowing and lending emerged, to poor effect. Companies like Celsuis, BlockFi and Genesis emerged as early leaders in this space. These companies operate like a bank but use cryptocurrency in place of government currencies. The existence of companies like this demonstrates how big, complex, and mainstream Bitcoin has become.

Bitcoin first emerged as an alternative to the traditional financial system. It flourished in the dark corners of the web. As it gains mainstream adoption, many believe it needs to be regulated. Proponents believe that regulation will increase market stability and investor confidence as well as create a safer ecosystem. Earlier adopters believed regulations would stifle innovation and would be against Satoshi's ideology.

Because of a series of market events in 2022, crypto lenders experienced major financial troubles and gained attention of regulators around the world. A downturn in the price of bitcoin and other cryptocurrencies led to many lending crypto to large lenders to withdraw, leaving the lenders in a financial crunch. The store of value argument for cryptocurrencies like bitcoin is intriguing but still may be too early to properly lend upon.

Bitcoin's Maturity into Store of Value

Gone are the days of the underground Cypherpunk, the Silk Road and the hobbyist miner from the early days of Bitcoin. Today, large corporations are seriously looking at Bitcoin as a store of value and a hedge against economic conditions like inflation. In 2020, the publicly-traded software company MicroStrategy announced that it had converted $250 million in cash to more than 21,000 bitcoin.

It was one of the first publicly-traded companies to convert its cash reserves into cryptocurrency. Companies like Microstrategy, Tesla and Coinbase own significant amounts of bitcoin, primarily with the strategy of holding it as a hedge against the inflation of cash. The thesis that bitcoin is a hedge against inflation has yet to be proven over time, but it's an interesting experiment.

Exchanging bitcoin on jump drives at Meetup groups - an early way enthusiasts used to conduct transactions - is in the distant past. It has since been replaced by rapidly growing financial instruments. The Chicago Mercantile Exchange, for example, has created bitcoin futures that allow buyers to invest in bitcoin volatility. Some see this as an indicator of adoption, while others view it as compounding volatility.

The Bitcoin Evolution

Bitcoin started as an idea. It became something that a global community eventually supported. Some of this was pent-up demand from cryptography enthusiasts, the Cypherpunks and the Libertarians. Other support came from the dark web. All of them contributed to the growing adoption of digital currency. In its early days, when it was cheap, bitcoin was used to make payments on the internet, particularly on the dark web. It's been through hard forks as different factions tried to decide for themselves the future of a network that is still being decided and created.

Today, the Bitcoin network hosts the world's most successful cryptocurrency, bitcoin. It's a distributed computer network powered by cryptography processing transactions. Many believe it's too big and entrenched to ever be stopped at this point. The reality is bitcoin is still a solution looking for a problem. It's not widely used as a payment method. Its market volatility sometimes makes it hard to define a store of value. Hard fork alternatives have also failed to gain traction. While Bitcoin may have come a long way from an idea, it still perhaps has ways to go.

In the End

Bitcoin set out to be a solution to the failed financial system. It envisioned a decentralized world where people controlled their money. This attracted an eclectic group of futurists and criminals. Together, they worked to build the world's largest and oldest cryptocurrency. Even with an uncertain future, one thing is clear... Bitcoin is not going anywhere anytime soon.

Things to Know From This Chapter:

- Out of the 2008 financial crisis the Bitcoin whitepaper was anonymously shared with the world, bringing forth bitcoin as we know it today

- Bitcoin was created with a finite number of coins that could ever be created by the system - totaling 21 million bitcoins

- The identity of Bitcoin has been unsteady - whether it's a store of value or payment system, challenged by slow transaction speeds to be a payment system

- Bitcoin has gone from its initial "dark web" reputation of unsavory users (like with Silk Road activities) to now being the network hosting the most successful cryptocurrency, bitcoin

Chapter Three

Ethereum

Satoshi Nakamoto's Bitcoin whitepaper promised a peer-to-peer electronic cash system. Through experimentation, early cryptocurrency pioneers identified the limitations of Bitcoin. These pioneers then forged their own path and built, in their view, a better cryptocurrency. The result became Ethereum and the concept of smart contracts, a foundational building block that allows for complex software to be built upon blockchains.

Bitcoin Network Constraints

As currently constructed, the Bitcoin network is not designed to handle a lot of transactions at the same time. It slows down when there are more transactions than can fit into a single block and fees become outrageous, pushing out those who can only afford low network fees. This only leaves the "whales". As individuals or entities that hold large amounts of bitcoin, whales have large enough holdings to manipulate cryptocurrency valuations.

The Bitcoin Core is a group of the main developers of the Bitcoin network. Their greatest concern is maintaining the network's security. For this reason, it is difficult to experiment with Bitcoin, and some people have left the

Bitcoin community to either start new hard forks of Bitcoin or start new cryptocurrency networks.

Bitcoin mining started as a hobbyist exercise. However, it has since evolved and has become an enterprise-grade business led by large companies. Every year, these companies spend hundreds of millions of dollars on chips alone. This has made it cost-prohibitive for regular people to be a bitcoin miner.

Bitcoin's Energy Use

The University of Cambridge Centre for Alternative Finance tracks the Bitcoin network. According to their research, at any given time, Bitcoin mining takes up 16.85 Gigawatts of power, the equivalent of 264 utility-scale wind turbines to power. Bitcoin consumes massive amounts of energy, which could be at the expense of the environment. This has long been a debate in the crypto community.

Bitcoin mining uses about 147 terawatts of energy per year. To give some perspective, just one terawatt of energy is enough to power 1.7 trillion light bulbs all at once. The scale and enormity of Bitcoin's energy consumption are immense. China, at one time, had over half of the share of mining, but the environmental impact was so severe that the government banned it altogether. Some experts think more state-led sanctions, regulations and bans around the world on Bitcoin mining are ahead.

There is a lot of work being done to build more transaction functionality on top of Bitcoin's software. In addition, many Bitcoin miners have supported greener energy. However, the challenges and flaws of Bitcoin have created new opportunities. That's why cryptocurrency pioneers are constantly building new protocols and Layer 2 applications that live on top of these cryptocurrency and blockchain systems.

The Ethereum Alternative

Many of the challenges facing cryptocurrencies forced early proponents of Bitcoin to look for a new system and build a completely separate blockchain. The most famous blockchain inventor is Vitalik Buterin, the co-founder of Ethereum. Buterin was a young and early advocate for Bitcoin. He wrote about the Bitcoin network for various crypto-focused media sites, and he began to envision something bigger and better. He called his new project Ethereum.

Ethereum is built on some basic tenets of Bitcoin but with many new ideas added in. Buterin wanted to create a blockchain that was a platform for software engineers to build on. Yes, there would be a cryptocurrency, but there would be much more. Ethereum would be a system on which anyone could build software applications, a feature Bitcoin does not have.

Buterin also had serious concerns about the future of Bitcoin mining as far back as 2013. He often criticized the energy waste that plagued Bitcoin mining. And yet, even though he criticized Bitcoin's energy waste, he implemented a similar energy-demanding mining system at the start. This controversy within the crypto community required major changes to Ethereum later on.

Ethereum's Whitepaper

In 2013, Vitalik released a proposal for Ethereum in a whitepaper. With the subtitle "A Next-Generation Smart Contract and Decentralized Application Platform," the paper excited early cryptocurrency enthusiasts. But what does that lengthy title actually mean? Vitalik put forward a new method of programming cryptocurrencies called "smart contracts."

This was an idea originated by academic and BitGold creator Nick Szabo in 1998. Smart contracts, powered by cryptocurrencies, would have particular legal arrangements embedded in the code. Many exchanges of money are legal agreements, and the goal of a smart contract, in theory, is to automate these processes with software.

If money can be digitized, why can't other real-world processes? Szabo theorized it should be possible to bring into the digital world legal functions that normally required lots of human effort and paperwork. For instance, escrow and liens, among others. Vitalik Buterin believed in this vision and set out to make it a big part of Ethereum's design.

The Vending Machine Concept of Smart Contracts

In essence, a smart contract is a computer program that can act as a vending machine. The first step is to insert money. In a smart contract, the money inserted is cryptocurrency. When using a vending machine, the user pushes a sequence of buttons to communicate and execute a command - insert money, push a button, get a soda. Similarly, a smart contract is fulfilled when its conditions are right - send crypto, smart contract executes and software for the user runs.

Buterin envisioned a decentralized application, or dapp, that would run the software. A dapp is an application built on a decentralized network like a cryptocurrency platform "d" for decentralized, "App" for software application. Bitcoin or Ethereum are examples of a decentralized network because no one single person or company runs them. The dapp concept basically combines a smart contract and a front-end user interface to interact with, like a web page or a mobile app.

Most applications people use, from email to social media and even stock trading, use a group of computers controlled by a third-party to operate. Bitcoin was designed to skip the third-party for financial transactions, while Ethereum's proposal was to do the same for financial transactions and computing power. An Ethereum smart contract must be programmed to tell it what to do in return.

A Turing Complete Blockchain

Ethereum was designed with "Turing-completeness," a concept developed by famed cryptographer and mathematician Alan Turing. It is a measure of a software programmer's capability to create whatever they want. Almost all programming languages used today are Turing-complete. Thus, a developer is free to create any logic needed to build a software program.

A Turing-complete blockchain is important. Because it allows for complex financial transactions to be completed without a middleman or third-party, such as the complex process of buying a house. Bitcoin was first in that it allowed for person-to-person payments with the blockchain as the verification. With smart contacts, there are much more capabilities than just payments.

One example of this: Buterin believed in the possibility of creating "colored coins," a real-world asset represented on top of the Bitcoin blockchain. However, Bitcoin has only limited capabilities beyond simple payments. What Buterin wanted was a regular programming language, Turing complete. This programming language could allow these colored coins to be used to represent real-world assets such as real estate. This colored coins concept would later become the foundation for non-fungible tokens, or NFTs, which would explode within the cryptocurrency ecosystem in 2021. Stay tuned, more about NFTs is discussed in chapter eight.

Colored Coins and Fungibility

Colored coins were first proposed in a white paper called "Overview of Colored Coins" by Meni Rosenfeld in 2012. The paper dived deep into the concept of bitcoin's "fungibility". As an asset, bitcoin has the ability to act like cash. Each bitcoin has the same worth and could be exchanged for another, making it what's known as fungible. However, "it is possible to color a set of coins to distinguish it from the rest," Rosenfeld wrote in his paper.

The same concept works for government-issued currencies. One dollar can always be exchanged for another dollar. This is an important concept that transfers over to cryptocurrency. There weren't very many other cryptocurrencies back in 2012 when the colored coins concept emerged. Many believed that the Bitcoin blockchain would be used for many different applications. Colored coins, for example, could provide non-fungible use cases.

The applications for both fungible and non-fungible crypto have many use cases. Some of these include issuance of shares, property rights and digital collectibles - which later became known as NFTs. Bitcoin, with its limitations, however, could not be the core platform for these types of blockchain applications. To act on these ideas, Vitalik Buterin and a group of technologists had to build a whole new system. Enter Ethereum.

Inventing the ICO

In 2013, the concept of the initial coin offering (ICO) originated with Mastercoin on the Bitcoin network. Mastercoin became a study of the capabilities of Bitcoin and explored new functionalities. It was created by software developer, JR Willett. Willett is also credited for providing the first ICO, raising around 4740 BTC (roughly $475,000) in 2013 using Mastercoin technology. ICOs are like the blockchain version of an initial public offering, or IPO, using this fundraising mechanism to fund its initial development.

Mastercoin is both a platform and a currency that was built on top of Bitcoin. It added features not included in Bitcoin's core software. This allowed for the idea of sophisticated programmable money. Mastercoin introduced the concept of complex software programs using blockchain technology. Mastercoin made it simple to create new cryptocurrencies, also known as "tokens".

Before Mastercoin, issuing new cryptocurrencies was only possible with software or hard forks. Buterin had lobbied the Mastercoin Foundation to add more functionality that programmers would need to build applications on its network. However, the Mastercoin Foundation was reluctant to make too many changes to its existing plan.

The Founding of Ethereum

Buterin decided to take things into his own hands, and so, with the help of another technologist, Gavin Wood, he set out to build Ethereum. It would be a separate blockchain, built with some ideas from the Mastercoin concept. The release of the Ethereum whitepaper in late 2013 brought a lot of excitement in the crypto world. In early 2014, Buterin announced the Ethereum project at a cryptocurrency conference in Miami, FL. Many in the audience had already read the whitepaper and were interested.

The Ethereum project had many co-founders led by Vitalik Buterin. These included, among others, Charles Hoskinson, Ethereum's first CEO, who later founded the cryptocurrency Cardano. Gavin Wood supplied technical expertise and later on founded rival Polkadot. Joe Lubin, a finance industry veteran, was in charge of marketing and later set up the consulting firm and startup incubator Consensys.

Ethereum set out to fund its project through the ICO fundraising mechanism. Many early Bitcoin proponents had enriched themselves by investing in cryptocurrency since it had gone from almost nothing to hundreds of dollars by 2014. Buterin knew there was an opportunity to get early "Bitcoiners" to invest in his project.

Ethereum's ICO

Ethereum offered Bitcoin investors an opportunity to invest through the initial coin offering or ICO method - a public offering opportunity to invest in a blockchain project. In cryptocurrency, a project raising money creates a new coin, application, or service and offers to early investors the new cryptocurrency at a discounted price.

The ICO is a funding mechanism that has fundamentally changed the way founders fundraised. Investors buy into an ICO to receive an ownership stake of a new cryptocurrency token. The token may have utility value or may represent a stake in the project. In Ethereum's case, it had both of these properties: The token, ether, would be used to pay for computing power, and represent the network as a valuable entity.

The Ethereum ICO was conducted through a Swiss nonprofit. After raising over $18 million from the community in BTC during 2014, the Swiss entity transferred those funds to the Ethereum Foundation, which has been the key provider of funding for development efforts.

Ethereum Fundamentals

The cryptocurrency used in the Ethereum network is known as ether, abbreviated as ETH. This cryptocurrency behaves like bitcoin and has similar transaction address nomenclature. Ethereum addresses start with the sequence "0x". This makes ether addresses easily distinguishable from bitcoin addresses (which start with a 1 or a 3). The Ethereum blockchain has much faster confirmation times, making it a quicker transfer mechanism than bitcoin.

Ethereum would create a decentralized "world computer," originally secured with proof-of-work mining, just like Bitcoin. Yet Buterin did envision an alternative to bitcoin's proof-of-work mechanism. In the beginning, Ethereum used a similar mining algorithm to Bitcoin called Ethash. But in 2022, Ethereum moved to a "proof-of-stake" security model (security verified by those who have crypto-based stakes in the system). This was an ambitious project that changed the Ethereum mining paradigm.

Ethereum has added capabilities when compared with Bitcoin. The platform takes cryptocurrency elements from Bitcoin to create software applications. That's why Ethereum has another unit of account called "gas," which enables developers to run what's called dapps, or decentralized applications, on the Ethereum platform.

Gas is the unit of measurement in Ethereum used to calculate miner payments for transactions. It is necessary because it rewards miners for processing transactions while defending the network against spam or cyberattacks. Gas is paid in ether. To keep the dapps running on Ethereum as efficiently as possible, gas is required to run software code on the network.

Early Ethereum Use Cases

During the early period of Ethereum's launch in 2015, use cases for the platform were few and far between. Later, software developers realized they could fund their own projects through ICOs - the same type of crowdfunding that launched Ethereum itself. Cryptocurrency could be raised in an automated and secure fashion using Ethereum. This made Ethereum the place to go for cryptocurrency pioneers and entrepreneurs to raise money for blockchain-based ideas.

As interest in ICOs grew by both entrepreneurs and investors, so did Ethereum. For example, a project that needed funding to launch could raise ether. In return, they could give donors a new, project-based redeemable cryptocurrency token built on top of Ethereum - using the same smart contract vending machine model described before. Investors speculated that those ICO cryptocurrencies, tokens, would grow in value along with the broader crypto market and based on the merits of the particular project.

During this early period for Ethereum, crypto-based fundraising had been gaining in popularity since the advent of bitcoin. In 2012, for example, entrepreneur Erik Voorhees raised money for his blockchain-based gambling site Satoshi Dice. Voorhees raised money by accepting bitcoin in return for digital "shares," proving this was a viable option and that there was a market appetite for these investments. In 2014, Voorhees was penalized by the Securities and Exchange Commission, or SEC, for conducting an offering like this without registering.

Interacting with Ethereum

The concept of dapps is based on the idea of distributed systems in computer science. Most apps that people interface with on phones and computers use a centralized system of management. In contrast, a dapp operates on a distributed system of computing resources. Examples of distributed systems include many telecommunication networks, including the internet itself.

Behind a website, for example, points to files as well as a centralized database that organizes and manages information. Every centralized website and mobile app follows this infrastructure.

Conversely, there are a few major methods for interacting with the Ethereum network. MetaMask is a browser extension crypto wallet designed to make accessing Ethereum's dapp ecosystem easier.

MetaMask makes interfacing with Ethereum possible for the average person, although there are other wallets that can do this too. Developers program their dapps to interact with a crypto wallet and smart contracts. They do this with a variety of tools, such as Web3.js. Another popular option is Infura. Using Infura offers developers a great advantage, as the learning curve to deploying products is much lower. However, the downside is it requires trust in Infura, a third-party, to pass along data. Alchemy is another option that many developers use.

Benefits of dapps

Ethereum's dapps make its blockchain more programmable and functional. A key feature of dapps is the lack of a centralized resource to power them, and they are generally found where there is a bottleneck in centralized systems. Many centralized apps, for example, are not censorship-resistant. This means on many centralized apps, a third-party decides what can and cannot be seen and used by users.

Often these types of decisions are subjective, arbitrary and made without input from users. Apple, for example, uses privacy as a decision-maker on a lot of policies within its App Store. Ethereum, in contrast, is the largest platform for developers to execute distributed code where arbitrary decisions from a third-party simply are not possible. This allows developers to deploy censorship-free applications.

Dapp platforms are still new. There's still lots to learn about how to create them as the infrastructure for doing so is still in its growth stages. One of the best sources of information regarding currently popular dapps is data aggregator DappRadar. Their website reports user numbers and cryptocurrency transaction volume for various dapps.

Discovering dapps

Many dapps listed on DappRadar are gambling, gaming and decentralized crypto exchange apps. Be careful spending cryptocurrency on these, as losing money is a possibility. There are several design challenges inherent to creating dapps today. This is an emerging technology, and as such, there are some drawbacks. Because of its distributed nature, tradeoffs exist when developing dapps versus centralized systems.

The speed of dapps relies directly on the speed of its blockchain and its confirmation times. This issue was perhaps most notable on Ethereum in late 2017 on the dapp CryptoKitties when its popularity led to an enormous number of transactions congesting the network. It's important to note that today dapps are not widely used. In fact, the traction and staying power of dapps are not yet strong, despite a lot of hype surrounding them.

Some issues with dapps include deployment, user experience, speed and scalability. These issues currently exist across all dapp platforms, including Ethereum. For dapps to gain greater market adoption, these issues will need to be solved. Perfection is critical in creating smart contracts for dapps. It is important to ensure software code does not contain critical flaws since it is not easy to deploy new contracts.

The DAO

Decentralized Autonomous Organizations (DAOs) were created to increase the distributed nature of Ethereum. Anyone familiar with creating smart contracts is able to launch a DAO. The intent of DAOs is to use smart contracts, the Ethereum-based software code, to replace centralized governance. This concept is similar to how the ICO concept replaces the centralized functions of an IPO.

As the name suggests, DAOs use a distributed governance system. In this system, stakeholders have voting rights commensurate with ownership of requisite tokens. The process is similar to how the voting and proxy process works for publicly-traded stock, but governance is done via smart contracts. The idea is to replace centralized third-parties in organizations and let the crowd make decisions with voting.

This decentralized governance concept was put to the ultimate test in an early Ethereum project known as "The DAO." In April 2016, The DAO was a smart contract-based ICO, designed to run autonomously, with investment decisions made based on the voting rights of token holders. The

DAO was able to raise over $154 million via Ethereum-based tokens from around 11,000 investors.

Despite its success in attracting investors, many vulnerabilities in The DAO were discovered. These vulnerabilities existed in the smart contract code, such as something called a recursive call vulnerability (RCV.). The vulnerability was known to some of The DAO's smart contract developers, but they were unable to update the contract's software code before an attacker deployed an exploit to take advantage of it. On June 17, 2016, this vulnerability was exposed when an attacker stole more than $50 million worth of ether from The DAO.

Ethereum's Hard Fork

The $50 million theft from The DAO and its investors led the Ethereum Foundation to make a tough decision. It had to hard fork the Ethereum blockchain. As the primary fundraiser and technical steering source for the platform, the Ethereum Foundation decided to create two distinct versions of Ethereum. The original blockchain that was hacked and the $50M stolen, is now called Ethereum Classic. The second, is a forked version that retracted said funds and returned the stolen crypto, is known as Ethereum. In this fork, the original funds could be returned to the investors who lost money in the hack by going back in the blockchain and splitting the protocol to reflect this new version.

Before Ethereum, the concept of hard forking a blockchain was considered taboo because of the concept of immutability. This is the idea of blockchain as a permanent and unchangeable source of data. It's a concept, even to this day, that many cryptocurrency followers still believe. The DAO hack enabled the community to warm up to the idea of hard forks.

Ethereum Classic is a blockchain that still exists today. Its developer community is much smaller and not nearly as robust as Ethereum. The Ethereum blockchain has been hard forked several times to accommodate for upgrades and unplanned vulnerabilities. Therefore, unlike other blockchains, many in the cryptocurrency world consider Ethereum not immutable.

The leaders steering Ethereum, namely the Ethereum Foundation and co-founder Vitalik Buterin, have no qualms in hard forking its blockchain. They favor experimentation and creation over hard rules like immutability. This is contrarian to the ideology of Bitcoin since immutability is often a priority. For this and many other reasons, the Ethereum and Bitcoin communities are often at odds with one another.

Ethereum Killers

It is still in the early days of the cryptocurrency ecosystem. Therefore, many tools and platforms need to be built before adoption of dapps increases. This is a great opportunity for innovators and entrepreneurs. And today, there are alternatives to Ethereum for building dapps, which will be discussed at length in the next chapter.

The Ethereum ecosystem started from just an idea in 2014 to a full-fledged global blockchain network. Smart contracts have incentivized many software developers to build on Ethereum or alternative "smart contract" blockchains. Some people call these alternative blockchains "Ethereum Killers". No matter the name, developers are largely working on these blockchains instead, further aided by the resources and tools constantly being created in the ecosystem.

Ethereum and Bitcoin share some core crypto concepts, but their advancement is clearly going in very separate ways. In its early days, Bitcoin was considered an all-encompassing technology. Then developers began to realize there were more features blockchain technology could support. Differences in ideology resulted in a new blockchain known as Ethereum.

In the End

Building smart contracts on a blockchain has enticed developers to flock to Ethereum. Yet the platform is not flawless. The network has had its constraints, slowing down or even refusing transactions to properly run dapps. Gas fees have often gotten out of control, costing hundreds of dollars for one transaction, all when transaction demand ramped up due to crypto markets skyrocketing in price.

Meanwhile, solutions to solve these issues bring additional complexity and security problems - and the Ethereum Foundation is actively working on these issues. Technical constraints led to the rise of the Ethereum Killers - Cosmos, Avalanche and Solana are a few examples.

Things to Know From This Chapter:

- Ethereum was designed to skip third parties for financial transactions and computing power

- Smart contracts are special software programs that enable applications to run without middlemen

- ICOs use smart contracts on Ethereum to raise capital for blockchain based ideas/projects, DAOs use smart contracts to replace centralized governance

- Ethereum has changed from a proof-of-work security verification system similar to Bitcoin over to proof-of-stake

Chapter Four

Stablecoins

There are thousands of cryptocurrencies. This book has already covered a few of the most innovative from a technological standpoint. However, there's a type of blockchain-based asset that deserves its very own chapter: Stablecoins.

This chapter will discuss the evolution of stablecoins, the challenges and their importance to the cryptocurrency ecosystem. Stablecoins are an evolving technology and understanding why they exist is essential.

Early Days

In the early 2010s, a market started to develop for bitcoin. This increased its price from almost nothing to being valuable. And early adopters were not just mining bitcoin, they were also buying it. However, the methods for buying and selling back then were pretty crude compared to today. Someone wanting to invest in bitcoin, for example, could go to a meetup, pay someone in cash, and get a digital wallet of coins. Not always a desirable process for people.

Early online services for bitcoin, such as BitInstant, founded in 2011 by Charlie Shrem, allowed someone to go to a bank, which seemed a little less shady, and provide cash to an account number. BitInstant, once having received the cash, would fill the order via its service, providing the customer with a digital wallet of bitcoin.

Still, the BitInstant process was clunky and wasn't a way people were used to interacting with financial services. Most people are used to bank accounts and online services such as PayPal. In the traditional finance world, these types of exchanges are known as "brokerage" or "over-the-counter" (OTC) transactions. Give someone cash and get an asset in return.

Cryptocurrency Exchanges

As the market for bitcoin grew larger, cryptocurrency exchanges started to emerge. Like stock exchanges, these services helped to match crypto buyers with sellers automatically. Customers would put in a "bid," the highest amount a buyer would pay for an asset. On the other side of the transaction, an "ask" is the lowest amount a seller would take in return for an asset.

Exchanges automate this process with software by assembling an "order book," where customers can place these potential transactions. A "matching engine" is software that pairs buyers with sellers, and vice versa. It's the way most markets work: People are matched up in a market without ever having to meet or verify each other before trading.

Cryptocurrencies like bitcoin are digital, and the customers are distributed worldwide. For this reason, digital exchanges have become vital for the trusted trading of cryptocurrency. Brokerages, like BitInstant, are simply too inefficient and localized for a decentralized global asset like bitcoin.

The Banking Conundrum

Mainstream stock market exchanges use systems that are connected to banks. People have to transmit government-issued money like dollars to a broker account when buying a stock. Then, investors can use a stock exchange order book to make a purchase or sale. Transferring government-issued currency in and out of crypto is where the problem with crypto exchanges began. Banks did not like these exchanges in the 2010s because cryptocurrency was considered a very risky asset class.

Banks that process payments must ensure that their clients are following all regulations; after all, customers that are facilitating money laundering or other illegal activities can cause a bank massive fines or even to lose its charter to do business. So for the most part, banks have just wanted to avoid cryptocurrencies, believing them to be too risky and requiring too much work to process crypto transactions. Banks do the same thing for various other industries: Cannabis, adult websites and gambling are examples of risky transactions for banks to process.

Simply put, if cryptocurrencies couldn't be easily bought and sold, the market and the asset value could not grow. In fact, many believed that it would be difficult for a market for cryptocurrencies to develop at all. Crypto exchanges could not rely on banks or government-issued currency. To solve this problem, early cryptocurrency advocates started thinking about ways to provide a stable asset inside the crypto ecosystem. So, why not just create a cryptocurrency that pegs to a more stable asset, such as gold, dollars or euros?

This is the basic premise of stablecoins.

Introducing Stablecoins

One of the first stablecoin projects was called Nubits, founded in 2014. The project created a monetary system, similar to how a central bank works, to create a stablecoin. This was considered controversial due to its potential to circumvent centralized government currencies. The idea behind the project was that its operators would control the Nubit cryptocurrency's supply and demand mechanics.

It worked like this: The project would have a reserve of bitcoins to back Nubits. Investors would put bitcoin into the reserve in exchange for a small profit. This reserve would then give Nubits value. To peg Nubits to $1, the project would alter demand and supply accordingly. At very a basic level, this is what a central bank does to control economic factors like inflation.

When inflation rises, central banks take money out of circulation. Conversely, when the opposite happens, deflation, central banks put money into circulation. This helps maintain a stable government-backed currency that people can rely on as a form of payment. Generally, at least in the U.S., this has allowed for the long-term average inflation rate of around 3 percent. That is pretty good, considering some government currencies have inflation rates five times as high.

Nubits Goes to Bits

Now, back to Nubits. If Nubits price point went below $1, the project would take some of the cryptocurrency out of circulation. The idea was that with less supply of Nubits, market demand would rise back to $1. Conversely, if Nubits were to go to a price above $1, the project would put more of the cryptocurrency into circulation, with the idea that more supply would get Nubits back to that $1 equilibrium the project was looking for.

As it would turn out, bitcoin's volatility was much too high to back a stablecoin. The project was unable to ride the waves of cryptocurrency volatility effectively. During 2014–2015, bitcoin remained relatively stable in terms of price. However, as the price of bitcoin began to rise in 2016, investors in Nubits demanded BTC back, possibly to sell or spend, breaking the peg. It happened again at the end of 2017 when the price of Nubits went as high as $1.50.

Having bitcoin as a reserve asset did not work for the Nubits stablecoin. What's more, the project was only "fractionally" backing the coin. While this is popular in the traditional banking industry, central banks can control the power of government-backed currencies via circulation levers. Nubits, on the other hand, was simply not able to do that. It would not be the last project to try this.

Fractional Reserves

Fractional reserves are popular in the traditional banking industry. In a basic sense, banks use the deposit money to make money as a business. Most prominently, bank deposits are used to make loans, and the bank profits by charging interest. Therefore, banks don't physically have - or - physically keep the entirety of customer deposits—the amount is "fractional."

This fractional approach has been used for decades, sometimes with disastrous consequences, as it was the main factor leading to the Great Depression in 1929. As people became concerned about the economy, a "bank run" occurred, and people rushed to banks to get cash for their deposits.

The classic movie "It's a Wonderful Life" does a great job of explaining this phenomenon. In reaction to the Great Depression, the U.S. government set up some laws to prevent bank runs in the face of fractional banking. This included the Federal Deposit Insurance Corporation, or FDIC, which insures U.S. customer deposits up to $250,000, among other measures.

Bitcoin and cryptocurrency emerged as a result of the 2008 global financial crisis. As a new financial system is being developed via cryptocurrencies, the participants are unfortunately perpetuating the previous pitfalls of conventional financial markets and banking. This will undoubtedly bring more regulatory scrutiny. Today, no regulations exist in the cryptocurrency industry for fractional reserve stablecoins. Primarily because cryptocurrency companies operate outside of banking rules and regulations, while cypherpunks, anarchists and the nefarious may desire to live outside of regulated markets, there is a reason why these regulations exist.

The Evolution of Programmable Money

In 2013, Bitcoin competitor Mastercoin launched. The coin started out as a software fork of Bitcoin, and it was designed to provide more functionality than the original blockchain. Many people look at Mastercoin as a precursor to Ethereum. In these early times, however, Mastercoin struggled to find a use case. It rebranded itself several times, from Realcoin to Omni. The concept of "programmable money" was one of the core tenets of Omni.

In 2016 there was still a need for a stablecoin after the Nubits experiment failed. The founders of Omni built a stablecoin called Tether, pegged to $1 US. Cryptocurrency exchanges like Bitfinex began trading Tether. Bitfinex had a particular interest in Tether as the exchange had struggled with banking. Remember, most financial institutions did not and still don't want to interact with crypto. The initial concerns lingered about money laundering and "dark markets" where people could buy illegal goods by paying with BTC gave Bitcoin a bad reputation.

In 2015, Bitfinex was one of the biggest cryptocurrency exchanges in the world. Yet the banking problem of getting actual dollars into its exchange proved to be very difficult. This made the concept of Tether quite attractive to Bitfinex: A dollar replacement that would allow the exchange to have a stable asset with which traders could use instead of volatile cryptocurrency pairs. For example, the ether/bitcoin pair was popular on exchanges, but it gyrated wildly—way too much for anyone with traditional finance experience to trade crypto.

Tether

Bitfinex wasn't the only early cryptocurrency exchange to adopt Tether. Many others did, especially those that had trouble with banking or resided in jurisdictions that could not obtain USD. However, Bitfinex's relationship with Tether was much closer than other exchanges. At some point, the two entities became closely intertwined, with executives from Bitfinex also running Tether.

Using the Omni blockchain early on, Tether says that it backed every single token (denominated USDT) to one dollar. It provided a transparency page on its website that matched the assets and liabilities to back it. But questions started cropping up, especially after 2016, when Bitfinex was hacked for 120,000 bitcoin. Tether also lost its peg briefly in 2017, dropping to as low as $0.92 before it recovered. Bitfinex was increasingly having banking problems, and in 2017, it sued the bank Wells Fargo for freezing money transfers, but later dropped the lawsuit. And, all this time, the amount of Tether in circulation was steadily increasing.

By June 2017, Tether's market capitalization had grown to $100 million. In July of 2018, Tether's peg rose to as high as $1.32. And while the token has remained relatively stable otherwise, the project's inability to get a full audit backing each Tether to an asset has led many to believe that, like Nubits, Tether may be fractionally reserved. Today, Tether is a huge influence on the cryptocurrency market, with tens of billions in market capitalization. Questions still remain about the company, including reports that it falsified documents in order to obtain bank accounts.

The Tether Bull Run

Academic research affiliated with the University of Texas has suggested that Tether may have had something to do with the 2017 crypto market bull run, as its market capitalizations in the last six months of 2017 rose from $100 million to over $1 billion. But then, Tether and Bitfinex paid an $18 million dollar fine to the New York Attorney General in 2021. It was revealed that the firm had borrowed hundreds of millions of dollars from an individual after it had been short of funding to back its stablecoin.

During the investigation, documents revealed that when it was short of money in 2018, the project's operators indicated the overall crypto market would collapse if it could not receive funding to pay out withdrawals. Since its founding in 2014, Tether has adopted several different blockchains other than Omni. Ethereum, Solana and many others now have Tether tokens on their platform. This is likely because the Omni protocol, like bitcoin, is slow, and new, faster blockchains have emerged since Tether's founding. In addition, the adoption of faster chains meant that high-speed traders could use USDT to move money around quickly.

Tether is a controversial project. The executives behind it have never really been able to dispel the concerns about it. It has never had a proper audit from an accounting firm. Most exchanges that use it to replace the dollar are not able to process USD properly due to lack of banking. Although its market capitalization is in the tens of billions, several reports claim that it has at times been fractionally reserved and not pegged one-to-one with a dollar for each unit of USDT.

With all of its controversy, Tether does solve a real problem within cryptocurrency. It provides liquidity and alternative banking features. Without these, the cryptocurrency market could not have grown to what it is today.

US Dollar Coin (USDC)

In 2018, a joint stablecoin effort was launched by crypto companies Coinbase and Circle. These are two of the longest-running U.S. crypto firms in the industry. US Dollar Coin, or USDC, is a stablecoin project that is paired one-to-one with USD. This means all coins in circulation would be backed by assets that could be verified in monthly statements. A consortium called Centre was formed to manage this project, and the coins were issued on the Ethereum network.

The project claims that it is backed by dollars or other financial instruments, meaning other stable assets, such as treasury notes. In 2021, the Centre website was updated to say the coins were "backed by US dollars" to "backed by fully reserved assets." The auditing firm Grant Thornton, LLP provides monthly attestations to the project's reserves backing the coin.

Both Tether and USDC are categorized as "centralized stablecoins." This means that one entity controls them. Bitfinex clearly controls Tether, while USDC is under the auspices of the Centre consortium. Neither of these two projects has actually been able to show a full audit, especially Tether, but USDC is generally considered to be the safer and more transparent of centralized stablecoins.

Central Banks and Stablecoins

USDC is an open-source project, which means that its software is available for anyone to review. And after its launch in 2018, many exchanges listed it as an alternative to Tether. USDC was built on Ethereum; it has become a big part of the decentralized finance, otherwise known as the DeFi market. It serves as a stable reserve to use instead of dollars on decentralized exchanges (DEXes) as government-backed fiat currency is not used on DEXes.

Sometimes, there is some confusion between USDC and Central Bank Digital Currencies (CBDCs), the latter being stablecoins that might be issued by a government and are a new form of blockchain-based asset. China is currently adopting CBDCs, and the U.S. Federal Reserve is looking into the technology as well.

Central banks are very interested in building their own stablecoins. After years of appearing as antagonists of blockchain technology, these institutions now see value in the technology's application. So it's only a matter of time before the stablecoin adoption by governments takes place. China seems to be the furthest ahead on this innovation as it has made moves to completely digitize the Chinese yuan renminbi.

Stablecoins as a Service

Tether, USDC and CBDCs can all be placed in a bucket known as centralized stablecoins; there is one entity that controls them. Another smaller competitor in this space is Paxos, a New-York-based firm that runs the cryptocurrency exchange itBit, which powers PayPal's crypto service inside its app. A PayPal user buying crypto is essentially using Paxos's itBit exchange.

Paxos operates a number of white-label (coins they create for others to customize and market) stablecoins. In essence, companies that need a stablecoin can use Paxos just like PayPal does for crypto exchange. For example, the exchange Binance, which has the BUSD stablecoin, uses Paxos as its technology provider. Paxos also offers USDP, known as the Pax Dollar. Between the Pax Dollar and BUSD stablecoins, Paxos has billions of market capitalization in the stablecoin market.

Another category is known as algorithmic stablecoins. This is a newer innovation where software is used to control the coin's stability. The ethos of decentralization and distribution, where no one entity can control a cryptocurrency, is one of the reasons why algorithmic stablecoins were created.

MakerDAO

The longest-running project in the algorithmic stablecoin vein is called MakerDAO. The term DAO stands for "decentralized autonomous organization". A DAO is a form of governance invented within the cryptocurrency community to build and foster distributed projects. The nature of this distribution requires some direction for a project to move forward, and DAOs can help to provide that with proper governance procedures.

MakerDAO was initially devised by Rune Christiansen, an early crypto enthusiast who recognized the need for a stable asset in the Ethereum ecosystem. Considered advanced for its time, MakerDAO's development led to an explosion in decentralized finance (DeFi) well after its founding in 2015.

The DeFi movement would not have been possible without stablecoins, like Maker's DAI entering the space. This stems from the cypherpunk ideology that prides itself on opposition to the mainstream finance and banking system that wants nothing to do with that ecosystem. This opposition bred the need for a unique crypto financial instrument, an algorithmic stablecoin called Maker DAI.

How MakerDAO Works

MakerDAO is smart-contract-based and has two different cryptocurrencies: MKR and DAI. MKR is the "governance token" within the system and is used to vote on various aspects of the protocol, such as what assets are used to "collateralize" or give the network value. DAI is the stablecoin backed by the collateral in the system.

It's essential to explain a few terms in the stablecoin or larger token ecosystem to fully grasp how MakerDAO works. "Minting" is the creation of new tokens. In terms of MakerDAO, a user can "mint" new stable DAI by sending cryptocurrency to its smart contract. "Burning", conversely, is the destruction of DAI by withdrawn cryptocurrency collateral from its smart contract.

The amount is "overcollateralized" in the Maker ecosystem to ensure the DAI is backed even during volatile times. This means the amount of DAI a user can borrow in the system is between 55%-75% of the collateral posted. When a user wants their cryptocurrency collateral back, they send back DAI so it is "burned" or destroyed from circulation. This is the basic algorithmic process that Maker uses to maintain a stable asset.

MakerDAO Collateral

When MakerDAO was initially launched, the sole collateral asset was Ethereum's ether token. Users would send ETH to the MakerDAO smart contract and receive the DAI stablecoin in return. The process could be reversed by sending DAI back to the smart contract and receiving ether. DAI has a market capitalization in the billions. The MakerDAO community, which consists of MKR holders, decides which cryptocurrencies are accepted as collateral. Since MakerDAO is an Ethereum-based stablecoin project, any type of token on that network could potentially be used. Other stablecoins, such as USDC, now make up a large portion of the collateral that backs the system.

But there are bigger things going on and the increase in USDC's prominence in Maker is due to these larger market effects. Stablecoins that depend on other cryptocurrencies, like MakerDAO, must automatically liquidate holdings in the event of a massive downward fall in prices. An example of this occurred in March 2020, when the price of bitcoin went to as low as $4,000 and ether slipped to below $90 briefly on some exchanges. In that event, the MakerDAO "liquidation engine" automatically started to close out positions to maintain the $1 peg of the DAI stablecoin.

Since that time, the MakerDAO project has, with community support of MKR holders, built in some new protections to help limit the number of liquidations that may have to happen in the event of a crypto market crash. This includes something called the "Emergency Shutdown Threshold" that would shut down the entire system and make DAI unavailable to redeem if certain market metrics are hit. Maker's DAI stablecoin has added significant value to the Ethereum and larger crypto ecosystem. Like all cryptocurrencies, it is learning as it goes. Only time will tell which will be the prominent stablecoin, but the MakerDAO has the foundation to be around for a long time.

Terra

Two categories of stablecoins have been covered here: Centralized, asset-backed stablecoins like USDC, and algorithmic stablecoins like Maker DAI. A newer category has also emerged called fractionalized algorithmic stablecoins. These assets use liquidation engines similar to Maker. However, they do not over-collateralize or even completely collateralize their assets but are only fractionally backed like banks. They operate similarly to banks—except they aren't regulated at all, with no oversight.

The most notorious of these is called Terra, founded by Do Kwon and Daniel Shin in 2018. The Terra project has two tokens: the LUNA governance token and the stablecoin UST. Like Maker, LUNA is a token used for voting on the particulars of the protocol. What makes it different from Maker and its MKR token for governance is that LUNA is also used to back UST, which is pegged to the dollar.

The "algorithmic" part of this ecosystem is what happened to LUNA when the new UST was created. When someone "mints" or creates a new UST, LUNA must be "burned" or destroyed. In this way, the system uses a form of arbitrage between tokens to back the value of the stablecoin. It is a fractional reserve but with one volatile asset in the form of LUNA. It also has bank-like properties and features. Terra used something called Anchor Protocol, allowing users to deposit crypto and gain a "yield" for doing so. This is the fractional backing for the reserve of the stablecoin. But unlike traditional banking, it was not regulated.

Anchor Protocol was giving people very high yields, much higher than would be found in a savings or money market account by bank account. Another appealing factor with Anchor: accessibility. Users could deposit U.S. Dollars and then receive the equivalent amount of Terra to obtain yield for depositing into the protocol. There's nothing implicitly wrong with these things, but in traditional finance, such opportunities are usually considered too good to be true.

Terra's Demise

It's likely that Terra's complex ecosystem, with two tokens and Anchor supporting an inflow of dollars, might have been too much. Cryptocurrency is like a science experiment. Each of the protocols and currencies is testing their theories in real-world scenarios. That means, unfortunately, the chance of failure is high.

Terra is built on the Solana blockchain, which has as its goal to be more high-performance than Ethereum. One of the use cases for Terra is to be able to move funds very quickly, which is something that a lot of traders require in the ecosystem due to the lack of dollar liquidity in the system. However, many people find these high yields appealing, especially when they can be up to 20% on average per year (APY) rates.

Some of this lack of dollar liquidity in the crypto market has actually made headlines. In 2022, Do Kwon told the media that Terra would buy $10 billion worth of bitcoin and that the project was already buying $125 million of BTC per day. The goal was to better help back the stablecoin, with the idea that bitcoin is less volatile than Terra, which has gone from about a dollar in 2019 to as much as $116 in 2022.

Not dissimilar to Nubits, however, Terra eventually collapsed. As the cryptocurrency markets trended downward in 2022, people began withdrawing money from Terra, which led to a "death spiral" with not enough collateral for the Terra stablecoin to remain pegged. Terra founder Do Kwon faces legal problems both in the U.S. and South Korea, his home country. Over time, the cryptocurrency markets have started to mirror the global financial markets. Innovations like Terra continue to push digital finance forward. Yet it is time that will ultimately tell which projects have value, usability and credibility for the long term. Terra is an example of one that does not.

Stablecoin Swapping

Other fractionally-backed algorithmic stablecoins have also suffered catastrophic crashes. Another example comes from 2022 with the WAVES stablecoin, called Neutrino or USDN. WAVES is an Ethereum-like blockchain, and USDN used the WAVES token to fractionally back its value. However, WAVES, which launched back in 2016, was not very popular and so only a few traders were using it.

This lack of support eventually led to its demise: WAVES, as a DeFi network, trying to compete with Ethereum could not maintain any stability; its token was volatile, and so its stablecoin lost its peg. Ethereum does not have this problem because it has many different stablecoins in the form of Tether, USDC and Maker. And in DeFi, it is possible to easily trade between all of these because they are all based on the Ethereum blockchain.

"Stablecoin swapping" is something that Ethereum-based smart contracts are built to do. Exchangers like Curve and others allow traders to easily go between each one, and this provides a pool of these assets for people to use. Solana has a similar ecosystem, as major stablecoins also use the Ethereum blockchain because of its speed and low transaction costs. Bottom line? It's hard to build an ecosystem around stablecoins. WAVES could not do it. Terra couldn't do it, Nubits either. Could another ecosystem succeed?

In the End

Stablecoins are the foundations of decentralized finance, a new system that largely operates out of the purview of traditional finance. And stablecoins are controversial because they provide similar services to banks but are not regulated, and banks believe this gives these competitors an unfair advantage.

It remains to be seen how governments will regulate, or perhaps even co-opt, stablecoins in the future. The technology to digitize things like the dollar are clearly being fostered. Imagine crypto that can represent these stable assets, or the euro or even other assets like gold. It's an exciting prospect for digital internet money, but also has been rife with dangers and collapse. Stablecoins are likely just the beginning of tying real-world assets into blockchain-based ecosystems, and that's an exciting prospect down the line as cryptocurrencies mature.

Things to Know From This Chapter:

- The stablecoin's premise is to create a cryptocurrency that pegs to a stable asset, like the US dollar, gold or the Euro

- Failures, hacks and fraud abound with stablecoins, and yet successes exist

- USDC is a stablecoin backed by US dollars and is a fully reserved "centralized stablecoin" with one entity controlling it and considered "safer"

- Stablecoins challenges are building an ecosystem around them, so time will tell if they are viable long term

Chapter Five

Markets and Derivatives

When bitcoin was only worth a few cents, people exchanged it using the peer-to-peer method. This method is still popular in under and undeveloped countries that operate on in-person cash exchange systems. Peer-to-peer is exactly what it sounds like. One person (a peer) exchanges a good or service for cash with another person (the other peer).

However, as time passed, the value and use of cryptocurrency increased. As cryptocurrencies grew in value, there was suddenly a need for more complex exchanges, markets and derivatives.

The Growing Need for Exchanges

Since banks didn't want anything to do with crypto in the earliest days, many cryptocurrency investors had a problem. The risk involved for banks to deal with an unregulated instrument like bitcoin was simply not worth it. Banks live comfortably off deposits and loan income. Why would banks take a risk on cryptocurrency? For the cryptocurrency industry to flourish, more sophisticated transaction methods were needed. To grow, it required the support of banking infrastructure, and it would also need to build tools similar to those used in traditional finance.

Cryptocurrency started and grew early on as a counterculture movement. However, it would need markets and derivatives, like regular finance, to succeed and have any chance at becoming mainstream. Big questions loomed: could cryptocurrency actually be utilized by a mainstream audience? Would large corporations accept and use cryptocurrencies in the future? In crypto's salad days, it seemed unlikely.

What is the difference between decentralized finance and traditional finance? Traditional finance is built on regulated, centralized database systems operating within banks and financial institutions. Whereas decentralized finance is based on cryptography, smart contracts and decentralized governance on the blockchain. It would take a new generation of innovators to develop this new finance system. And crypto exchanges, some of which are ironically centralized, were a big part of getting everything off the ground.

Mt. Gox

An early crypto exchange company was called Mt. Gox. The name came from the game Magic: The Gathering. The exchange's singular name was an abbreviation of Magic: The Gathering Online Exchange (MT GOX). Many people would say it like this: "Mount Gox." Founded by software developer Jed McCaleb and later sold to entrepreneur Mark Karpeles, Mt. Gox was one of the very first cryptocurrency exchanges. For a time—the most popular, and then eventually, perhaps one of the most controversial prior to FTX (with its own shocking widespread scandal and fall in 2022).

Mt. Gox was originally founded in 2010. At one point, it processed over 70% of all global BTC transactions. In 2014, Mt. Gox suddenly suspended its trading, shutting down its website and exchange services. It also filed for bankruptcy protection from creditors and began liquidation proceedings. The exchange ceased operations when it was revealed it had been involved in the loss and/or theft of hundreds of thousands of bitcoins. At the time, lost bitcoins were worth hundreds of millions of dollars. In August 2015, Mt. Gox CEO Karpeles was arrested on charges of fraud and embezzlement.

Of the 650,000 missing bitcoin, 200,000 bitcoins were recovered. Initially, the reason for their disappearance was unknown. Wizsec, a Tokyo security company, concluded that most of the missing bitcoins were stolen out of the exchange's hot cryptocurrency wallet over a three-year period. Crypto exchange and brokerage security have come a long way since 2014, but one still must be aware of the risk that still exists.

Brokerages Versus Exchanges

In a brokerage, transactions are usually run by a third party. An exchange uses technology to match buyers with sellers, while brokerages usually do this manually. A "matching engine" is software that helps buyers find sellers and vice versa. Matching engines for cryptocurrency exchanges are unique software.

The crypto market runs 24/7 and can have high trading volumes at any time. Stock exchanges have trading hours, whereas crypto exchanges run continuously. Many who work in these markets often say that "crypto never sleeps," and it is an accurate depiction. Crypto exchanges aren't unlike stock exchanges, though.

All crypto exchanges operate on a "bid" and "ask" system. A bid is the highest a buyer is willing to pay for an asset, an "ask" is the lowest price the seller is willing to accept. Exchanges, with their matching engines, use software code to facilitate these transactions, ensuring the buyer doesn't know the seller and vice versa. Trust comes from the exchange itself, how and who operates it and there are certainly varying levels of trust in crypto exchanges.

Exchange Order Types

When a trader places a bid or ask, it is known as a "market order." Once a market order has been placed, the matching engine goes to work to find the best bid or ask. There are many more complicated order types that traders use, with every exchange offering different options.

The most common order types come from those available on traditional stock exchanges. Another popular order is a "limit." A limit order specifies executing a price that is at a certain level, whether that is a buy or a sell.

For example, a stock trader might want to buy or sell an asset for a price of $100 or more. This person would put in a limit order for $100. Once the currency hit this price, the order would automatically be executed. A stop order is a type that executes automatically at a specific buy or sell price. Hence, the name "stop" because a trader is essentially "stopped" and the order is automatically executed. Traders can also specify something called "good until canceled." They can also set specific parameters for when an order might expire.

Keep in mind that the type of orders on a crypto exchange can be very different from one exchange to the next. Stock market traders may be used to things like limit and stop orders. If these aren't available for active trading, this can be quite problematic. For example, a crypto trader would not want to put in an order and then have to watch it until execution. Stop and limit orders allow a trader to set the parameters for their buy or sell order. Without these features, a trader would either have to track the order or be at the mercy of the market.

Different Cryptocurrency Exchanges

Some traditional stockbrokers use crypto brokers. These brokers facilitate cryptocurrency trading on their platform and only offer market orders. It is really important to be aware of the types of orders exchanges offer before starting to trade. Getting stuck in an order that can't be easily unwound is problematic; the cryptocurrency market is volatile and notorious for big price swings.

People are amazed when they find out there are thousands of different cryptocurrencies. What many do not know is there are hundreds of cryptocurrency exchanges. Each exchange offers something a bit different. The data aggregator CoinGecko, for instance, lists hundreds of exchanges.

When it comes to cryptocurrency exchanges, there are three different types: Centralized, decentralized or derivative. Centralized exchanges are the most popular in the cryptocurrency market today and are run by companies that develop matching engines. There are hundreds of centralized exchanges on the market today, and they can vary wildly.

Decentralized exchanges (DEXes) allow for users to trade cryptocurrencies directly with each other without the need for intermediaries or central authorities. Lastly, cryptocurrency derivative exchanges are platforms specifically designed for trading derivative contracts based on cryptocurrencies, and allow traders to speculate on the price movements of cryptocurrencies without owning the underlying assets directly.

U.S. and Europe Exchanges

Coinbase, Kraken, and Gemini are the three largest (and also oldest) U.S. exchanges. Each offers a different set of blockchain-based assets, order types and other features. In Europe, Bitstamp is generally known as the primary cryptocurrency exchange. The main reason for the variety of exchanges that exist is regulatory jurisdictions.

Each country and often even subregion has different laws about cryptocurrency. Exchanges often need to be located in the jurisdiction they serve. In the United States, cryptocurrency exchanges must adhere to state and federal law. In particular, money transmission laws must be followed.

The U.S. exchanges have money transmitter licensing in states that require them. Each state often has different requirements. In New York State, for example, cryptocurrency exchanges are required to get a certification known as a BitLicense. Two of the three largest exchanges (Coinbase and Gemini) have a BitLicense, whereas Kraken does not.

Exchanges Outside U.S. and Europe

Outside of the U.S. and Europe is a very different landscape for centralized exchanges. Since the many regions (in Asia, Africa or South America perhaps) are not dominated by one currency like the U.S. (the dollar) or in the E.U. (the euro), most of these exchanges rely on stablecoins instead of government-backed currency, with stablecoins taking the place of government-backed currencies. Many of these exchanges eschew banking altogether in favor of blockchain-based stablecoins.

Binance is a leader among centralized cryptocurrency exchanges and has some of the highest trade volumes thanks to its use of stablecoins. However, the exchange has had various jurisdiction and banking issues, including some uncertainty about where the exchange itself is actually domiciled.

There are a lot of exchanges like Binance that rely on stablecoins, using them in lieu of government-backed currencies. Converting investments into government-backed currency may not be possible on these types of centralized exchanges. This is why as an investor, it is important to do proper research before using a particular exchange.

Over the Counter (OTC)

In 2017, a new venue for trading became popular—over-the-counter (OTC) trading, a mixture of brokerage and exchange. During a bull market in 2017, there was a demand for large buys and sells of crypto. These orders were much larger than what a regular brokerage or exchange could handle, transactions generally higher than $250,000.

There was a reason for the rise of OTC trading platforms in 2017. The ICO boom resulted in large amounts of money converting into Ethereum-based tokens. "Slippage", the difference between the expected price of an order and the executed price, made it hard to buy or sell any amount of crypto over $100,000 on exchanges during this time.

Companies like Circle jumped into the OTC business. For a time, Circle was one of the biggest traders in this space. It worked like this: A buyer or seller of large amounts of cryptocurrency would call an OTC desk. They would say, "we want to sell $1 million of bitcoin." The OTC desk would then quote a price that would expire at a specified time, for example, 10 minutes. Once the timeframe expired, a new quote would be required for the transaction.

Crypto OTC Desks

Cryptocurrency OTC desks can usually fill orders quickly. OTC desks have existing relationships with large investors that are actively looking for discounted deals, and so they use these relationships to fill buy and sell orders. Circle was a large exchange, wallet, and brokerage in 2017. This allowed them to capitalize on the opportunity to make money as a desk. Today, this service is provided by crypto exchanges, hedge funds and large brokers. Naturally, these service providers usually bake in a fee into the quoted price.

Across the board, larger crypto orders are actually more expensive to execute than smaller ones. There is usually no "bulk discount" for these services due to the effect large orders can have on the market at any given time. The crypto market has grown exponentially, but it is still relatively a small asset class when compared to traditional finance. Despite its growth, single entities still have the ability to shift the market price.

OTC providers follow the same regulatory framework as brokers and exchanges. These regulations serve as a safeguard against fraudulent activity. Regulatory compliant OTC desks ask for know-your-customer information, often referred to as KYC. In order to review sources of funds, the OTC desk will often look at blockchain analytics, a topic covered in-depth in later chapters.

Fundamentals of Markets

Another type of exchange is of the decentralized variety. As the name might imply, decentralized exchanges, or DEXes, don't have centralized order matching. These exchanges use smart contracts, many of them Ethereum-based, to match bid/ask orders. Decentralized exchanges are the cornerstone of decentralized finance, or DeFi.

The main premise of DeFi is that smart contracts can replace the need for a trusted third party. In conventional finance, banks and other financial institutions serve as the credible middleman, while decentralized exchanges use stablecoins and tokens to perform this role. The DeFi ecosystem believes that technology is less fallible than humans.

Ethereum's ERC-20 standard is a big part of decentralized exchanges. Ethereum's tokens are all built on the same platform, meaning these cryptocurrencies can be "swapped" in decentralized exchange. Oftentimes, the term "swap" is used when trading in and out of different cryptocurrencies in DeFi.

Wrapping in Decentralized Exchange

There are methods to allow non-Ethereum cryptocurrencies to take part in decentralized exchange. One concept is called "wrapping." In wrapping, a cryptocurrency is locked in some way using a smart contract of multi-signature address, which is a safeguard to prevent the asset from moving. The value is then utilized on another blockchain like Ethereum while locked up.

Wrapped cryptocurrencies provide interoperability, meaning, the crypto asset can be used on blockchains to which they are not native. The most prominent example of this would be wrapped bitcoin (wBTC). Bitcoin holders can "wrap" their bitcoin and trade it on the Ethereum platform using a special wallet. Ultimately, the asset stays on the BTC blockchain.

The beauty of wrapping has brought bitcoin and other cryptocurrencies to smart contract platforms such as Ethereum. This increases the utility and liquidity of smart contract platforms and DeFi applications. Other reasons to wrap cryptocurrencies may include ERC-20 token swapping, which allows the crypto asset to take advantage of blockchain functions that it might not have on its native chain.

Slippage on Decentralized Exchanges

Decentralized exchanges (DEXs) have less liquidity or trading volume than centralized exchanges. Lower trading volumes cause DEXs to have "slippage", with traders often seeing their buy or sell orders "slip" to an undesirable price point. However, while more prominent on DEXs, slippage can occur on any exchange, even traditional stock exchanges. But the lack of a centralized order matching engine with DEXs can cause trading to be slower than other exchanges. In the fickle crypto market, this can mean traders don't get as good a price as they might on a centralized exchange.

DEXs have dealt with this problem by deploying automated market makers, or AMMs. A common concept in centralized exchanges, market makers provide the service of order matching, which results in increased trading volume and liquidity. In the conventional markets, makers match buyers and sellers for a fee. On a DEX, the market maker is a function automatically facilitated. It is a feature often created by a DEX's software development team since this matchmaking can increase liquidity for both buyers and sellers.

Many decentralized exchanges started out with the concept that anyone could use them, so there wasn't a plan to verify customers using know-your-customer rules. This anti-money laundering practice is common on centralized crypto exchanges since know-your-customer (KYC) and anti-money laundering (AML) practices are required in conventional financial institutions. DEXs do not use government-backed money, and so there has been a belief these exchanges could forgo KYC and AML practices. At some point, regulators will likely intervene as a lot of fraud and other nefarious activity can occur on exchanges that don't identify their users.

Bull, Bear, and Crypto Winter

At this point, it's important to explain the bull vs. bear mentality in the markets - this concept exists in traditional markets as well as in crypto. A bull is someone looking at a market positively, and is considered "bullish." A bear is someone looking at the market negatively and is considered "bearish." The cryptocurrency market goes through cycles just like all markets, and they are similarly identified as bullish or bearish.

Again, this is also true with stocks and other financial markets, but crypto has its own dynamics. The cryptocurrency market generally runs hot, cold or prolonged periods of low market activity. There are three general conditions in the market: bull, bear, and "crypto winter". To better describe this, it's important to go back to when the crypto exchange market was starting to mature starting in 2012. At that point, there were lots of sources to buy or sell cryptocurrency. In 2013, there were two bull cycles, one in April and another at the end of the year.

In 2014 and 2015, the market went into a crypto winter - a prolonged period of low price action, before gradually gaining steam in 2016. By

2017, a large bull market appeared, followed by another, albeit briefer, crypto winter. Things started to pick up in 2020 before a huge bull market developed in 2021. By late 2021 into 2022, a bear market emerged, which appears to have developed into another crypto winter.

The ETH/BTC Pair

As this illustrates, the crypto markets are notoriously fickle. The price of bitcoin has steadily increased over the past decade. And when bitcoin does well, other crypto assets do too. Crypto traders like to call this "altcoin season," a time when the price of bitcoin does so well that most investors will diversify into other assets.

Many traders watch something called the ETH/BTC pair. This pair is popular on many crypto exchanges. When the market is bearish, many traders will sell ether for bitcoin because they see it as a safer reserve asset. When the market is bullish, traders will sell bitcoin profits to diversify into ether. It's a nice indicator of where the market is at because neither asset is stable at any given time.

Ether started to really take off in the previous 2021 bull run, with many other crypto assets benefiting too. It remains to be seen whether ether will be able to stand alone as an asset. As the second-largest cryptocurrency by market cap, it has made impressive gains. Yet, it still seems to often, but not always, track bitcoin price-wise.

Derivatives Markets

One other component of crypto's market infrastructure is derivatives. In traditional finance, derivatives are considered to be complex, but the crypto world is much more basic than Wall Street at this point. One type of derivative is options. An option is a right, but not an obligation, to buy or sell an asset by a particular time. That time is known as expiration. Basically, options traders make bets on price movements in a particular time period.

For example, an options trader may want to bet that the price of bitcoin is going to $75,000. The trader would then make a bullish trade, known as a call option. They would set an expiration date and designate the price amount to call or exercise that trade. A trader thinking bitcoin will drop to $10,000, would buy a put, which is therefore a bearish position.

Another popular derivative is futures. This instrument is used to bet on the future price of something. It is very popular in the commodities markets. For example, a farmer will try to lessen the risk of their upcoming corn crop yield by purchasing futures. By locking in a favorable price ahead of time, no matter what happens, including the weather or other adverse factors affecting that yield, the farmer lessens the risk.

Cryptocurrencies have futures instruments, too. In the US, commodities are regulated by the Commodities Futures Trading Commission (or CFTC). The CFTC has said that both bitcoin and ether have properties of commodities. Regulated bitcoin futures trading began in 2017. Ether futures trading started in 2021 on the Chicago Mercantile Exchange, or CME. For example, purchasing futures allows bitcoin and ether miners to "hedge" against market risk, in order to reduce or offset their risk.

Derivatives are highly regulated instruments, especially in the United States. There are many derivatives exchanges outside of the United States. In the United States, financial markets are regulated by the Securities Exchange Commission, and the SEC is still hesitant to approve most cryptocurrency derivatives.

Exchange Traded Funds (ETFs)

ETFs are a popular financial instrument in the stock market. They allow investors to own exposure to many different assets outside of just stock. These include commercial real estate and commodities like gold and oil. For example, an investor can buy into commercial real estate by buying an ETF on the stock market associated with owning such properties.

There are several futures bitcoin ETFs available on the US market today. These derivative instruments allow investors to speculate on the future price of BTC. In Europe, investors can buy a crypto Exchange Traded Product (ETP), the European version of the ETF.

There have been efforts to get a "spot" bitcoin ETF approved by the SEC, but none have succeeded so far. A spot ETF invests in bitcoin at its spot price. This means ETF buyers would be holding bitcoin within the fund. Many crypto enthusiasts view spot bitcoin ETFs as a more direct path to crypto, opening up consideration for it to be a legitimate investment option. Meaning, safer. And many in the crypto market think that the SEC's avoidance of approving spot bitcoin ETF is wrong.

Many financial firms have applied to offer a spot bitcoin ETF, to no avail. The SEC has issued guidance that there is not enough transparency in crypto for a spot bitcoin ETF. Cryptocurrency has long attempted to operate outside government regulation, and the SEC's primary concern is protecting the majority of investors. The SEC clearly does not believe that cryptocurrency, as it exists today, has a place in mainstream finance.

Bart Simpson Pattern

It's important to remember that the crypto market is still quite young. And it is not regulated like traditional markets are—at least not yet. One of the most glaring examples of this is a phenomenon known as the "Bart Simpson Pattern" - which regularly appears in the crypto markets.

Crypto traders are highly aware of the Bart Simpson pattern, which occurs when the price of bitcoin or ether goes up significantly. This price holds for some time - and often then goes right back to its previous price (the visual graph looking a lot like Bart Simpson's head outline). It's not like something like this couldn't or wouldn't happen in regulated markets, but it rarely does. While this event occurs with a good amount of frequency in the crypto markets, it is not entirely known what causes these patterns.

Some speculation is that unregulated exchanges themselves create these patterns to burn crypto margin traders. Others believe that crypto 'whales,' large investors, are creating these patterns for personal gain. Regardless of who is causing these patterns, regulators believe that these are indicators that the crypto market is quite different from regulated markets.

Liquidations

Another concern about the crypto markets is the issue of liquidations. Some exchanges outside the US and Europe - again, usually unregulated - allow traders to take massive amounts of leverage. This means they are borrowing to make huge trades. Leverage can magnify profits - but also can mean massive losses.

The problem arises when markets begin to dramatically rise or fall—or a Bart Simpson Pattern occurs. At this point, traders get automatically "liquidated." As price moves against them, crypto exchanges will automatically close their positions. Crypto traders can experience strange patterns, over-leverage, unexpected liquidation and exacerbated prices. It's not for the faint of heart.

Investing and trading cryptocurrency is complex, and many traded crypto assets experience continual, often relentless, volatility. Since "crypto never sleeps," the market is ripe to move at any time. Often, there will be higher-than-usual market moves during strange hours. These hours can also include holidays, where traditional markets would be closed.

Bitcoin Stocks

Without surveillance and better controls, the SEC will not approve a US spot crypto ETF. However, that hasn't stopped some publicly traded companies from buying bitcoin and acting as a proxy for a spot bitcoin ETF. Instead of an ETF, investors can buy some of these publicly traded company stocks and get exposure to bitcoin in that way.

The best example of this is MicroStrategy. It is a publicly-traded company on the NASDAQ (MSTR) with the highest bitcoin holdings. MicroStrategy has almost 130,000 BTC, while miner Marathon Digital (NASDAQ:MARA) has 10,000 bitcoin. Crypto exchange Coinbase (NASDAQ: COIN) holds 9,000 BTC, while payments company Block, formerly known as Square (NASDAQ:SQ) owns 8,000 bitcoin.

These companies see bitcoin as a store of value alternative to cash. As of 2022, the dollar has seen significant inflation. The U.S. Federal Reserve seeks to keep inflation around 3 percent per year. From 2021 to 2022, that rate was more than double, at 7 percent. Publicly-traded Companies that would normally hold a lot of cash are turning to crypto as a cash alternative, and they are doing this despite blockchain assets having a large volatility risk.

In the End

The crypto markets are globalized, fast-paced and fascinating. The early days of crypto required a community to back it. Now, there are tons of tools and players - even publicly traded companies are investing in crypto!

These players are starting to understand and embrace the possibilities of cryptocurrency. A market for blockchain-based assets is continually growing, no matter what the price of cryptocurrencies may be in a given day.

Things to Know From This Chapter:

- There are many cryptocurrency exchanges - several paths exist to trade/buy crypto via these exchanges

- Areas around the world have exchanges backed by stablecoins instead of their regional government fiat currencies (whereas in the US exchanges are backed by the dollar and the E.U. exchanges are backed by the euro)

- Market orders can include puts, stops, futures with "slippage" being an important issue to contend with

- Smart contracts replace trusted 3rd parties with decentralized exchanges - so it's the trust in the technology or blockchain that comes to the forefront

Chapter Six

Smart Contracts and Security

Despite all the fascinating technology of cryptocurrencies, they are very much people-controlled. A user must start a transaction, check their balance and stay vigilant of security practices. In the early years of crypto, this was pretty much the entirety of the ecosystem.

Software developers could see potential, though. They had seen this potential long before bitcoin's invention, and the academic researcher Nick Szabo was one of these people.

Programmable Money

In 1996, Szabo wrote "Smart Contracts: Building Blocks for Digital Markets". He laid out the concept that contracts - like the ones used in the legal profession - were "the building blocks of a free market economy." This includes contracts for both business, like employment contracts and for relationships, like marriages.

Szabo may not have known it at the time, but this concept worked well within the realms of blockchain technology that developed with Bitcoin later on. For example, Szabo's paper detailed the concept of mutual contracts executed without a middleman and instead using software to automate it.

In his section on "Contracts Embedded in the World," Szabo explored the idea that many technologies had already acted as a form of contract. The section "Cryptographic Building Blocks" explains much of the basic theory behind cryptography and discusses its potential use for smart contracts. What's fascinating is, Szabo wrote this a decade before cryptocurrencies even got off of the ground.

Ethereum Smart Contracts

Ethereum was one of the first major platforms to develop and launch smart contracts. Today, it is only one of many, but it retains the most traction among software developers. Ethereum's founders set out to create a "world computer" that would allow programmers to build applications that are much more complex than cryptocurrency systems like Bitcoin.

Smart contracts are software code that allows the cryptocurrency to be programmed so that it becomes much more than just a new store of value or payment system. It opens up a plethora of opportunities for what cryptocurrency can be used for (estate wills, loans, escrow services, financial instruments, for example) - all the while removing the need for middlemen and centralized governance.

Smart contracts can also put into place communities that can help guide the project. This is especially important given the distributed nature of some cryptocurrency projects that have no one party or leader that controls the system. This type of governance is known as decentralized autonomous organizations, or DAOs, and these are powered by smart contracts.

Legality of Smart Contracts

It's important to keep in mind that smart contracts don't represent any type of enforcement by law or the legal system. Szabo's concept was to use software to perform real-world contractual enforcement - but that part of the idea has still not been totally figured out. Removing third parties is a core tenet of smart contracts. This is done to remove human biases, errors, and expenses, by getting rid of a third party that seeks rent or taking a cut of transactions.

Free speech may be another reason. It can help a political party or an unpopular view, for example, avoid being susceptible to censorship. Large corporations use data for purposes that are unclear to many users, and so by removing third parties, such as Google, Facebook and Amazon, you can help protect user privacy significantly.

These companies sell customer data to brokers who then use the information to target their ads better. However, the idea that "Code is law" in smart contracts has been dispelled by lawyers who specialize in the subject of blockchain and cryptocurrencies. It remains to be seen how courts and legal systems in the world at large will interpret smart contracts.

Smart Contracts and Web3

Crypto, blockchain and, in particular, smart contracts, can help remove expensive middlemen because smart contracts enable users to control more of their data. This feature has the potential to displace existing large technology giants, which harness user data for business purposes. Many people don't realize this, but the world of the web today is often known by technologists as "web 2.0," the second generation of the consumer internet. The consumer internet is a place where users can do things like blog, check email and use social media; with everything taking place inside of an easy-to-use browser.

Web 2.0 is different from the world of "web 1.0." This was the beginning, when the internet was static, used most for reading information by academics and early internet adopters. Creation in the web 1.0 world was much different than 2.0 as it often meant having to develop a website, which was difficult for most people to do. Web 2.0 emerged as the second generation of the consumer internet in the early 2000's - this is why it's called "2.0". During this time, many companies like Google, Amazon, Facebook, Twitter and Apple have become giants in the "tech" sector. Often these groups of companies are just called "tech" or "FAANG," short for Facebook, Apple, Amazon, Netflix and Google. Yes, there is an acronym for everything.

But many don't realize how much of the internet these companies actually control today. Google, for example, controls over 87% of the search engine market. It is the largest domain name service (DNS), a crucial service for websites. Google's email service, Gmail, is the largest in the world, with 1.5 billion users. Every day, Google processes 20 petabytes of data, which is 20,000,000 gigabytes per 24 hours. For comparison, most new iPhones today come standard with approximately 128 gigabytes of memory.

The concept of "web 3.0" means a world where the power of the web is owned by the individual user. Today, the web consists of 5 billion users who appear to be at the mercy of tech giants. Large tech companies have been able to harvest the value of these users in data, which is used to bombard users with programmatic advertising and other gimmicks.

Smart Contracts and DAOs

Smart contracts are software systems that need minimal user information and identification. Today, consumer data is stored in the databases of huge technology companies. Users sign terms and conditions agreements giving these companies rights to ownership and control. Thanks to these agreements, the big tech companies have pretty much the right to do whatever they want with this data.

Smart contracts seek to give some ownership and control back to the user. Also, smart contracts allow digital communities to build on top of software. This gives people some ownership of a project, which seems like the complete opposite of providing free personal data to a big company.

Decentralized autonomous organizations, or DAOs, power these communities. These DAOs allow communities to vote on a project's direction. This is important because the consumer web can be thought of as an autocracy. Each Big Tech company can be thought of as a ruler that creates its own arbitrary rules. Web 3.0 can be thought of more as a true democracy that seeks to give power and governance to the people.

Governance and DAOs

This DAO structure is often known as "governance" in the crypto world. While it is not perfect, it could enable people to have a larger stake in the technologies they use. This is in stark contrast to big technology platforms that give users no power or little say.

One good comparison to this is the traditional startup company equity structure. In startups, founders and employees are given stock options for taking the risk of joining an early-stage firm. Advisors are usually given some equity as well. Customers may also be given stock options or discounts. They receive these incentives for the risk of working with unproven technology or business. Later, when it's more established, customers do not receive these incentives.

In a DAO, equity or customer discounts come from a cryptocurrency - these are often known as project tokens. Smart contracts assist in this process by allowing token holders to make organizational decisions. Voting rights correspond to the number of tokens held. This is similar to voting rights in publicly traded companies. The Gitcoin project is an example of this. Gitcoin is designed to incentivize people to work on software projects, mostly in the crypto space.

The Gitcoin DAO has a token, called GTC, that community members hold to vote on projects. The idea is to build public goods in the software and blockchain space, powered by its own community. Today, while it is almost impossible for the average person to be able to avoid using big tech, there are some like Gitcoin making it easier for people to circumvent the FAANG (Facebook, Apple, Amazon, Netflix, Google).

Early Smart Contract ICOs

A disdain for big company data ownership is at the core of the smart contract ethos. Like many ideas in the crypto space, the creators of smart contracts want to give some technology power back to the people. Smart contract platforms like Ethereum had the funds to take off thanks to ICOs.

ICOs function on the "vending machine" concept. The buyer inserts crypto into the smart contract address, and in return, the smart contract spits out a new type of crypto to the buyer. It was one of the first and most important uses of smart contracts. The ICO concept has been likened to a vending machine because it automated the process of buying a stake in a project. The smart contract took the place of a middleman seller or broker.

And unlike traditional markets, anyone in the world could at first buy into initial token offerings before regulators stepped in and asked projects to start capturing identification for users. Regardless, the ICO can be thought of as a "vending machine" version of an initial public offering (IPO) on a public market. Many early ICO projects found success. For instance, the prediction market Augur raised over $5 million for its Ethereum-based token. However, that's not to say all projects early on were as successful in raising funds.

The DAO

In 2016, a project known as "The DAO" launched an Ethereum smart contract to raise funds. The DAO espoused the ideals of distributed governance, and it had very little formal structure. The funds that were sent to the smart contract by investors in The DAO and were controlled by a group of multiple private key holders, otherwise known as a multisignature address.

This means no one person controlled it and group consensus was required to make changes via use of these keys. This distributed structure was attractive to crypto and technology advocates who wanted to fund new projects; both for- and non-profit. In return for investing in the DAO smart contract, investors were provided DAO-specific cryptocurrency tokens.

Some investors only wanted to invest the funds in bitcoin and no other cryptocurrencies. Other investors were seeking to diversify their crypto assets and saw The DAO as a prime opportunity to do that. Many enterprising projects pitched their ideas to The DAO community in hopes of receiving funding.

The DAO Flaw and Ethereum Classic

Members of the community noticed some flaws in The DAO smart contract, including one that pertained to something called "recursive flaws." Inevitably, the smart contract was hacked using a combination of the noted code flaws and this recursive flaw problem. The hackers withdrew approximately a third of the ether in the contract. At the time of the hack, it held more than 11.6 million ETH—approximately $50 million.

The hack caused a community uproar. This caused the developers of Ethereum to perform a hard fork. As mentioned before, a hard fork splits a blockchain. The goal of this hard fork was to return the money lost to hackers to their original owners. The developers went back and forked the chain before the hack, returning user balances. As a result of this fork, the original chain (as mentioned in a previous chapter) is now known as Ethereum Classic or ETC.

Today, ETC is listed on many exchanges. Owners of ether before the fork received the amount of ETC that mirrored their ETH holdings at the time of the fork. While ETC might have originated from the ether, the two assets have very different prices. And while many have talked about blockchains being "immutable" or unchangeable, this hack showed that a community around a blockchain can decide to make changes in unforeseen circumstances.

In 2017, a year after the hack, the Securities and Exchange Commission, or SEC, did a report on the DAO. It deemed DAO tokens a security and, therefore, subject to federal securities laws. The acceptance of ether for

DAO tokens did not meet the standard of a crowdfunding exercise because the project was not registered with the SEC.

Projects used smart contracts under the guise of "crowdfunding" to circumvent established SEC fundraising laws. In the SEC's DAO Report, the agency stated the importance of the U.S. being at the forefront of innovation while admitting that raising money this way could be problematic. The SEC believed that the ICO fundraising mechanism had legal implications for its originators. In addition, it was clearly a large risk to non-accredited investors who may not understand the dangers of crypto.

Increased Security

Another problem was the security problems inherent in Ethereum at this time. The founders of Ethereum wanted the platform to reach large-scale adoption, and because of this, there were very few security guardrails in place at the beginning.

In centralized technology systems, security systems are placed to prevent software vulnerabilities. In building new software, developers can make mistakes that can potentially make it vulnerable to hackers. It's important to put in place a framework for such instances. This can include the "syntax", or the way a software language can be used in a system.

This is why system administrators lock down certain elements of technology. They require things like authentication access for certain pieces of information. Systems usually have several environments that software code must be pushed through before going live. These environments can include development, test and production. Sometimes many more can be included, depending on how critical a system is.

The important thing to wrap your mind around is how smart contract code is developed and run. So, blockchain technology is distributed, which makes it vastly different from centralized systems. Distributed systems rely on a system of decentralized computer nodes spread around the world. Centralized systems, by contrast, use owned or leased data centers - are much more controlled environments.

Blockchain Sandboxes

Around the time of the DAO, computing giant IBM helped to create a software fork of Ethereum called Hyperledger Fabric. This allowed centralized system administrators to safely play with Ethereum's technology. A type of safe computing environment is often referred to as a "sandbox." The sandbox environment could be locked down from a security perspective. This meant organizations that were afraid or concerned about blockchain technology could safely experiment.

Blockchain technology exists in two worlds. The first is a world that has been referred to as the "Wild West." This is the world where Bitcoin was created to usurp financial institutions. It is a place where people take on large risks in the hopes of making big profits. Many hope to take down the establishment and make the world a better place. Today, this world still tries to live outside the world of rules and regulations.

The second is the corporate environment. These organizations live within the constraints of rules and regulations. They have built large global brands that are fiercely guarded. While the organizations are often risk-averse, they recognize that if they do not embrace the technology it may eventually replace them. With open blockchains like Ethereum, corporate experimentation was not possible. These types of blockchain systems always have something called a "testnet," which allows developers to deploy smart contracts and try new things.

Composability

The biggest problem of blockchain sandboxes, however, is a technical issue called "composability," this is when a system is able to operate with other systems. The ability to operate across many blockchains could also be called interoperability. Composability allows one smart contract to interoperate with another, and it can be hard and very complex to test.

In most technology systems, software goes through a process to remove "bugs." This process removes flaws before it goes live to users. In the smart contract world, the process is different. Smart contract developers build their code and use independent auditors to review it before the "deployment" on a public blockchain for use.

Getting a good smart contract auditor is not an easy process. In a world of open blockchains, auditors can cost $250,000 or more to thoroughly review smart contracts. There is often a long wait as other projects are being reviewed. Many developers bemoan this fact as they believe that open software should not need an expensive auditing process. But getting the best auditors to take a look at the smart contract code is important. Savvy blockchain users only want to use smart contracts that have undergone a proper audit. With that being said, an audit isn't exactly a stamp of approval that a smart contract is completely safe.

There have been well-known audited contracts, for example, that have had problems. Many of these issues come back to this idea of composability. A drawback of the open-source blockchains is that these systems often don't work well together in spite of interoperability being a core tenet of their design. Because of this, there are some companies in the smart contract space that are building software systems to automatically audit and check code.

Oracles

Another issue of smart contract systems is in relation to data. In order for smart contracts to operate, they need an incoming stream of verified data. Traditional organizations rely on centralized databases as an information resource. Because smart contract systems aren't centralized, this database structure doesn't work in a decentralized fashion due to the distribution of blockchain systems. For example, many smart contracts need the price of ether updated on a real-time basis since most smart contracts run on Ethereum gas, therefore this updated price is vital.

Because smart contracts don't have databases of their own, they rely on distributed data sources known as "oracles". Smart contracts need some sort of trusted data source. This source can be from a trusted external party, or even an internal source created by the smart contact developers. Whether internal or external, the data needs to be trusted and verified... which is the most important element.

Internal oracles are known as centralized and are controlled by one party. This means they can have one point of failure if not set up in a distributed way. Many believe centralized oracles don't fit the ethos of the blockchain space. It is important to research the oracle data source before interacting with a service. The most important element of oracles is the quality and consistency of the data.

Since the launch of Ethereum, a series of oracle systems have originated. Some projects use external oracle sources, while others opt for an internal system. Externally-developed oracles are known as decentralized oracles. These oracles run independently of centralized authority. Chainlink, Band Protocol, Maker and Augur are examples of decentralized oracles, although none are alike and offer different data services to smart contract projects.

Gas and Smart Contracts

As outlined earlier, gas is the fee paid to a blockchain network to interact, and the prices are different depending on the type of transaction.

Gas plays a huge role in the entire smart contract ecosystem. It is an important gauge of the use of contracts. As outlined earlier, gas is the fee paid to a blockchain network to interact, and the prices are different depending on the type of transaction.

A simple address-to-address transaction on the Ethereum platform using the ETH cryptocurrency is the cheapest. There are variable fees depending on how fast a user wants to be placed in the blockchain. For example, getting a translation into the next block is the most expensive. A one-block delay is usually cheaper. Generally speaking, the longer the wait, the cheaper the transaction. Using an ERC-20 token to transfer is a bit more expensive, as it requires a little more smart contract power on the network.

Smart contracts that use much more mining power on the network, as a result, are much more expensive. Using a decentralized exchange contract, for example, is more expensive than a simple transfer. A lending protocol is even more expensive than a decentralized exchange transaction. Selling an NFT at auction is even more expensive than a lending transaction. The more mining power used, the more gas required. There are resources to see what gas prices are for various actions on websites like DeFi Prime and Ethereum Gas Station.

Gas prices vary and depend on many network factors. One is the price of the underlying asset, which in the case of Ethereum is ether. Another is the amount of resources required by the network. Finally, the number of people using the network affects the prices. More people using the network is usually when prices are also up. This can also make gas prices go up.

EVM and State Machine

The purpose of Ethereum's advent was to provide a "world computer" system. Coupled with cryptocurrency and blockchain, it changes the way many people think about computing.

Big tech companies offer software developers computing power, often known as "cloud computing." These tech companies control the systems. Therefore, they can make any changes at any time, and charge tremendous government-issued currency fees for these services.

Ethereum is unlike those cloud services. It uses something unique, called the Ethereum Virtual Machine, or EVM. The EVM is one large computer maintained by a distributed group of computers, known as miners, that provides something called a "state machine." This is where Ethereum's smart contracts exist when they are deployed or go live.

The state machine holds all ether holders' account addresses and balances. It does this using a special data structure called a Modified Merkle Patricia tree. A smart contract is like an account on the Ethereum network. Similar to a user address, it also has a public key. It's important to remember that a smart contract is like an account itself on Ethereum with a public key and private key. This is how users interact with smart contracts - by sending and receiving crypto from the smart contact's address.

Tools for Smart Contracts

What's great about this technology is that anyone can develop a smart contract. It does cost some gas fees as well as some software development skills, but the ecosystem is open for technologists to play with. For Ethereum, there are two special languages, Solidity and Vyper, for programming these smart contracts. While Solidity is the most popular, there are also some more developmental languages called Yul and Fe that are still in early stages.

Developers also need to use "frameworks" to build and test smart contracts, with Truffle being the most popular. There are many other software developers familiar with the Java or Python programming language, so it is easier for them to create code in an environment they already know. This is why developers also use software "libraries" to develop smart contracts.

Having a "node" into the network is important. Nodes connect directly to Ethereum, they interact with blockchain data on the network itself. Services like Infura, Alchemy or CloudFlare do this automatically. Miners also provide nodes, although the Ethereum network has gone through a major upgrade that has switched it from proof-of-work over to proof-of-stake.

Proof-of-Stake and Smart Contracts

In proof-of-stake, miners "stake" balances to provide computing power to a blockchain network. This is different than Bitcoin's proof-of-work, where there is no balances required - just computing power - in order to support that network.

The Ethereum Foundation provides the guidelines for the development of the network and worked on the upgrade to proof-of-stake for years. This allows Ethereum to process more transactions, in particular, to process more smart contract transactions. The popularity of the network has caused it to become slow and increased the price of gas fees - hence the upgrade.

To make the migration from the old Ethereum to the new, a "beacon chain" was built. The beacon chain allowed ether holders to begin moving ETH from the original blockchain to the new one. Users moving to the beacon chain "stake" their ether there. They can earn a proof-of-stake yield or small profit for doing so. The ether cannot be moved back to the old chain once it is moved to the beacon chain.

Since the advent of Ethereum, many blockchain-based smart contract systems are now live. These include Solana, Avalanche, EOS, BNB, and many others. For the most part, these competing systems offer similar functionality as Ethereum. These systems make it easy for developers to use. Most of the fundamentals explained here apply to these other networks.

Many of these blockchains already offer features coming to the new version of Ethereum - for example, proof of stake. This is what is motivating the Ethereum Foundation to move to an upgraded version of its network. And Ethereum keeps moving. Ethereum will also adopt "sharding," the process that will allow for pieces of computing to work in tandem and weave them together. This increases the number of transactions that can be conducted at a single time.

In the End

Smart contracts were an idea implemented early on by Ethereum. Ethereum network's open nature has inspired many new smart contract platforms to arrive. This gives developers an opportunity to choose from an array of platforms.

Today, there is a wide array of software for cryptocurrency users to interact with. They come in the form of decentralized applications and decentralized finance. All of which are covered in the next chapter.

Things to Know From This Chapter:

- Smart contracts are special software that expands cryptocurrencies into more than just store of value and payment systems

- Smart contracts seek to give some ownership and control back to the user, but they do not currently represent legally enforceable contracts

- Flaws and hacks plagued Ethereum's early implementation of smart contracts, leading to a hard fork of the platform and the creation of Ethereum Classic

- Smart contract outside audits are hard to get and expensive, creating the potential for vulnerabilities

Chapter Seven

Web3 and DeFi

S atoshi Nakamoto shifted the thinking around finance and technology when he released the Bitcoin whitepaper. The whitepaper envisioned a world where people were not completely dependent on financial institutions. However, early adopters soon learned that the Bitcoin network had limitations as a payment network and springboard for software applications. So Ethereum set out to build a platform for that.

The smart contacts and security chapter outlined that while Ethereum is not perfect, it has created a place where crypto innovators can play. This playground has allowed innovators to build new ideas, such as web3 and a new financial network called DeFi.

web3

Ethereum and smart contracts enable software developers to create decentralized applications. These are applications that do not rely on centralized services like most apps. In order to achieve this, developers circumvent the constraints of centralized systems using a system of distributed "protocols."

This is an evolution from Bitcoin - which upended the way people thought about value on the internet. Previously, only banks and governments controlled the store and transfer of value via fiat currency or dollars. Bitcoin began chipping away at that ideology and changed how many understood money, value and finance.

Today's software developers have a huge array of tools to create web and mobile applications, but many of these tools rely on big centralized corporations in the tech industry. For instance, Google and Amazon make up the majority of the server hosting industry. Using smart contract technology, software developers code, compile and deploy applications on blockchains.

These are known as decentralized applications, or dapps. This software runs on a decentralized system of nodes, and since they operate outside of a centralized system, they may be central to the future of finance and the greater ideals of web3. At its core, web3 is software running on a blockchain. It is a series of smart contracts that are operating with one another. The goal is to provide a consistent user experience, just like traditional software applications.

Web3 and Open Source Software

To further illustrate, let's take Microsoft, a software company most people are familiar with. Many people use Microsoft products like Windows, Office, or Xbox 360. When using Microsoft software, users are completely reliant on the company. Microsoft could come along and make unpopular changes to the software, and it's certainly done so in the past.

The company could charge more money for the product or start using personal data inside the software to sell ads. The software most people use is under the control of a corporation that could do anything it wants to on a whim. If the company is public, its primary interest is profit for its shareholders, while the needs and wants of the user are secondary.

With web3, a lot of software is "open source," meaning the smart contract software is available for others to copy and use as they see fit. If a decentralized application does something users don't appreciate, developers can simply take the code and create something new. Open source is not a new concept, it has been popular for decades. Many existing technologies use open-source code with the support of programming communities, including companies like Google, Amazon and even Microsoft.

The difference here is that dapps are smart contract-based, open-source software built with blockchains and cryptocurrencies, very different from how Microsoft usually builds its software. Web3 can encompass many different technologies built with traditional software today, such as games, gambling, social media and many other applications.

Decentralized Finance (DeFi) and Web3

A subset of web3 is decentralized finance (DeFi), an important part of the ecosystem. DeFi is basically a dapp that has financial functions and services. They help to run the entire dapps ecosystem. It brings the concept of financial services to users that want to be "crypto natives." These crypto natives don't want to take part in the traditional finance industry.

People use DeFi for a multitude of reasons. Some do not have good access to traditional financial services. Others use DeFi for ideological purposes, for instance, due to their distrust of traditional banking. There are also those who use it to bypass regulations found in regular banking and markets. Regardless, DeFi dapps allow users a unique way to operate outside of traditional banking rails.

This is done using smart contracts to automate the systems that usually require third parties. It even removes centralized crypto services, including exchanges and hosted wallets. There are smart contract-based crypto exchanges known as decentralized exchanges (DEXs) which provide control to the end users with "self-custody" wallets and the ability to hold their own private key.

DEXs operate using stable assets in place of government-issued currency, the primary use case for stablecoins. Stablecoins allow DEX users to trade and pair crypto-only assets with something stable. This could be gold, government-backed currency, bonds, or some other stable asset. But for ease of use, most of these stablecoins are backed by USD.

Stablecoins and DEXes allow smart contract developers to build more DeFi services, including lending, derivatives, and market-making. These are services that traditional finance usually performs to provide a marketplace. And this enables cryptocurrency to be used in dapps and the greater web3 world to come.

Infrastructure of DeFi

Stablecoins, like MakerDAO, provide the stability that volatile cryptocurrencies cannot. Decentralized exchanges like Uniswap provide a way to "swap" or exchange tokens. There are stablecoin-specialized DEXs like Curve to move from MakerDAO's DAI to USDC. There is even a lending market that allows existing crypto holders to borrow against their assets. This is all powered by smart contracts.

Some question the concept of borrowing against a volatile asset or other facets of the DeFi world. Nonetheless, the demand for these DeFi services is high by those who are well versed in the crypto and blockchain world.

This is because many people who hold crypto would rather do so than sell it to re-enter the traditional financial system - the crypto natives.

There are many reasons for the crypto native mentality, but some of the motivation comes down to taxes. Crypto holders don't want to execute a taxable event on their crypto, so they prefer to hold it. Or, the value of their cryptocurrency is below the price they paid. This is called "underwater," meaning the price paid is below the current market value. These reasons have produced a lending market for crypto, and growth in lending. There are also centralized services that provide crypto lending. The DeFi version provides unique services that centralized platforms do not provide.

Flash Loans

One peculiarity of the lending market in DeFi is the concept of "flash loans." It leverages smart contracts to allow crypto holders to take out loans and then return them. It works like this: A borrower contacts a flash loan lender for an amount needed, say $100,000. The lender then sets up a "receiver" smart contract. The lender sends the $100,000 to the contract.

The receiver contract now has $100,000. The borrower now controls the opening transaction and can use the funds however they wish, for instance, send them to other addresses or trade it on a DEX. While the funds have been received without collateral or any customer identification verification, the open receiver contract requires the return of the funds as it is still in a transaction state.

The entire process will fail if the $100,000 is not returned to that contract, requiring the original receiver contract to return the funds to the lender. The whole transaction is reversed as if it did not happen. Instead of collateral, the smart contract system automates the return of principle as the entire process must actually be mined into a block to be complete. After all, this is a core fundamental aspect of cryptocurrencies.

A transaction is not complete for as long as it's not mined. The design of flash loans reverts the whole process back to the lender receiving the funds back. It's important to remember this happens fast. Oftentimes, the borrower uses software to do this, so the whole process is done in a "flash."

MEV

Within DeFi, smart contract developers are able to pull off some pretty interesting feats. They can do things that are not possible in the traditional financial world. This includes, among other things, refinancing a debt position on the fly. Or conducting multi-asset arbitrage. That is, making money off the price difference between different crypto assets.

However, there are some intricacies to this process that can get gummed up. Blockchains are open and visible to everyone. Someone could see things like flash loans before they are actually mined into a block. Block times, the "stamping" of transactions permanently, happen at regular and planned intervals.

Some smart contract developers have engineered a way to see these transactions. They can see these flash loan transactions, for example, before going into the block. This potentially allows them to see these things, copy them, and change them. This dynamic is known as Miner Extracted Value (MEV) or Maximum Extracted Value. No matter the name, this phenomenon is likely not going anywhere due to the construction of Ethereum's system.

Yield and APY

The dynamics of lending are interesting within the realm of DeFi, and the way lenders are able to provide funds to borrowers is also fascinating. In traditional finance, banks lend money from a pool of deposits. This means the money people put into savings or checking accounts is "rehypothecated"—used for lending. Today, those with funds in a checking or savings account receive minimal benefits.

Banking customers are provided some peace of mind that their money is safe, along with a pittance of interest in return. This is usually denominated in average per year (APY) terms. In the DeFi world, cryptocurrency holders are paid a premium for providing funds that are used for lending and other uses like liquidity on DEXes. This means a pool of assets is available to trade on these platforms.

In return for offering up funds, holders get a "yield"—return on their assets— in the token provided or one offered for the DeFi service. This is known as "liquidity staking," or being a "liquidity provider," or simply being an LP. For the most part, these yields are higher than traditional banking, but there is certainly increased risk.

How Yield in DeFi Works

Here's a great illustration of yield. Uniswap, one of the most popular decentralized exchanges (DEX), always needs liquidity. This can also be described as an available pool of assets necessary for users to trade. High-interest rates are given to crypto holders who put assets into a smart contract so the funds can be used for liquidity. Uniswap provides a return for the period the assets are "staked" in the DEX.

This staked principle is true for many other services in DeFi; it's one of the key underpinnings of the ecosystem. Essentially, DeFi users are supplying the crypto that runs these services. This removes the need for a third-party like banks to facilitate - smart contracts do this work instead. For example, the lender Compound offers a variety of yields for crypto holders to stake their assets.

This allows Compound to have a pool of assets to lend out to users. Other services across the DeFi universe offer this as well. This includes derivatives platform dYdX, which offers many complex instruments for crypto traders. Stablecoin-only DEXes, such as Curve, are another example; providing specialized swapping of stable assets in the DeFi ecosystem. This list goes on, and because these dynamics are still pretty new, creative smart contact developers are coming up with new ideas for this all the time.

Layer 2

Services like Uniswap, Compound and dYdX are examples of smart contract-based DeFi applications. They live on top of what is referred to as "Layer 2." It's important to discuss this here because layer 2 has DeFi implications, both from the standpoint of usability and from the dynamics of staking and LP.

The price of Ethereum gas is correlated with platform usage. As more Ethereum is used, the price of gas increases. This has created in the past a situation called a "fee market," where people compete to buy gas, which is denominated in ether, for transaction activities. When there are a lot of people using Ethereum, or most other smart contract platforms, the blockchain actually bogs down the platform. Blockchains often have an inability to handle lots of transactions. Therefore, layer 2 applications that move beyond a base chain for faster and cheaper transactions were created.

Services like Polygon are an example of this. Crypto holders are rewarded for staking on Polygon, and moving assets there reduces network clogs on Ethereum. DeFi has been steadily growing. Ethereum in particular has worked on better ways of handling the issue with its upgrades. However, the reality is that layer 2 may become an essential piece of the blockchain world as the ecosystem grows to include billions of users over time.

Yield farming

DeFi users often define the value of a service with a measurement called total value locked (TVL). The TVL metric is the amount of crypto held in the service via smart contract. It's not a be-all-end-all source of information for DeFi services, but it's a useful measure. It also helps to understand something called "yield farming."

Yield farming is the practice of moving funds to the highest rate APY that can be found. It's a cat-and-mouse game. These users, known as "yield farmers" are on the hunt to find juicy returns in the form of APY while the TVL balance is low. There are TVL aggregators out there that track these balances.

It's a cycle that is repeated in DeFi over and over. A new DeFi service launches but doesn't have users or liquidity. To entice users, the service offers very high returns in the double-digits. Once the yield farmers are amassed, it brings in other users because of the high TVL. The most popular DeFi services have billions of dollars worth of crypto locked in their smart contracts.

Lockup Versus No Lockup

There are TVL aggregators out there that track smart contract balances. Dappradar, for instance, follows all the smart contract platforms available, not only Ethereum. It's important to keep in mind that yield farming is different from staking in smart contract platforms. Smart contract staking often requires a lock-up period. This means there is a time period for when funds must be deployed for the staking process and are not available for withdrawal. Examples of this include Solana, Polkadot and Cosmos.

Yield farming can offer big staking and liquidity provider opportunities for crypto holders. Nonetheless, it's a constant game. Yield farmers are always looking for better yields to stake. Without lock-ups, they are free to go ahead and put funds in whatever they choose and at any time.

However, this may not always be good for users as it can mean poor smart contract security. This can lead to hacks, scams and loss of funds. Yield farming is possible because these smart contract services, whether it is a DEX, lending, derivatives or something else, often lack a lock-up that many blockchains have.

DeFi Information

Since DeFi is distributed and decentralized, it is difficult to regulate DeFi. It's a real wild west environment for finance. And there's been a lot of opportunities for hackers and scammers to swipe money from the system. A good rule of thumb for using DeFi is to focus on the name brands that have good TVL. This is because many DeFi services are more flash-in-the-pan opportunistic types of services.

DeFi innovation has the ability to change finance as it is known today and help create a more inclusive financial system globally. Like everything in the crypto space, however, it moves very fast and is plagued with bad actors. It's best to only deploy money that one can afford to lose.

Sites like Instadapp are helpful. The platform lets interested users deploy funds into different services. It does this without a lot of smart contract work or cost. And there are a lot of research resources available like Dune Analytics and Token Terminal.

It is important to note that outside of the name brands mentioned, most DeFi services do not have longevity. This is because the ecosystem is still relatively small and yield farmers move from service to service, which affects TVL. One thing these DeFi services can do is increase their staying power by having a community. These communities are often implemented and run using decentralized autonomous organizations (DAOs).

How DAOs are Different

Unfortunately, the disparate interests of the community members some-times affect DeFi and web3 projects negatively and stifle their progress. Democracy gives people rights but doesn't always make it easy to govern or lead to quick decisions. It's important to keep in mind that DAOs don't operate like individuals. They don't act like corporations.

DAOs are unique entities. They proliferate as a result of cryptocurrency, blockchain and smart contracts. Within DAOs, there are subcategories. There are "protocol DAOs" like MakerDAO and "investment DAOs" like ConstitutionDAO, for example. An ever-growing list of DAOs includes gaming, social, and collecting.

In the realm of hardcore DeFi, Lido DAO is a popular DeFi service. Lido DAO works like Instadapp in that it allows users to use crypto funds across several services. When one engages in staking on Lido DAO, tokens are distributed to users in return for their stake. These are known as Lido Staked Ether, or STETH, which tracks with the price of actual ETH.

Examples of DAOs

The DAO, a smart contract-based system for investing created in 2016, was hacked due to security issues and poor code. However, it did not affect the concept of DAOs as they have since proliferated. Communities are important in the DeFi and web3 world because they give users a sense of ownership. A DAO provides its community with governance and voting rights via staked tokens. These voting rights are granted in proportion to owned shares in the token. The ability to vote on the direction of a token project creates a sense of ownership and loyalty.

That being in mind, DAOs are still very much in their infancy. One of the oldest and well known in DeFi is the stablecoin project MakerDAO - considered a "protocol" because it has a blockchain, token and pegged asset. MakerDAO started out as a centralized organization before converting to a DAO structure.

An interesting actual play involved ConstitutionDAO in an effort to buy a copy of the U.S. Constitution that was available at auction in 2021. It was an investment-oriented group like The DAO (with better code of course) to pool together funds from 17,000 investors. ConstitutionDAO was outbid by an individual bidder, Citadel hedge fund CEO Ken Griffin, for $42.3 million.

Another relevant example is called "grant DAOs", for example, Gitcoin. The platform is used for funding the development of open source code in the cryptocurrency world. Donors pursue a list of open source projects on Gitcoin and fund them using cryptocurrency. Software developers are paid in crypto when milestones are completed.

Wrapping, Burning and Minting

There are several tokens in the cryptocurrency market that are like derivatives. These are called "wrapped tokens". The most popular are wrapped bitcoin (wBTC) and wrapped Ether (wETH). They have been created to surpass technical limitations - the fact that cryptocurrencies exist on different blockchains. Bitcoin, for example, is on a separate blockchain from Ethereum.

Because of this, users are able to take BTC and place it on the Ethereum network. This is done by "wrapping" it into an ERC-20 Ethereum standard that can be used in DeFi. Ether also has this problem because the cryptocurrency itself is not an ERC-20 token standard for DeFi. It is the cryptocurrency used to do things like pay for gas required for computation on the network. Thus "wrapped" ETH exists as well so that it can be traded with other ERC-20 crypto tokens in DeFI. This ensures everything can be translated into the same blockchain language.

These wrapped assets are locked within their own chain in some way to prevent transactions and counterfeiting. This is often done via a smart contract. Meanwhile, the wrapped version of the asset is "minted" or created on the new chain. Conversely, when the token is sent back, it is "burned." Burning and minting are crucial to this new crypto world. What's important to know is that minting means creating new tokens while burning means destroying them. The ability to take crypto assets across chains opens up a world of possibilities.

Gaming and DeFi

The world of web3 isn't limited to DeFi, but it is a core component that makes other dapps like gaming work. This is leading to the rise of play-to-earn video games. These games are built on the fundamental infrastructure of DeFi. It's led to an influx of new users that don't necessarily know anything about DeFi. They only want to play games and earn cryptocurrency in return. Axie Infinity is often considered one of the first well-known popular play-to-earn crypto games.

Games like Axie need systems to scale to a large number of users. Axie Infinity users slay monsters, build things and find treasures within the game to earn tokens. As a result, the need for layer 2 systems has come into demand. This has necessitated the need for something called "bridges," which is a blockchain gateway to another blockchain. Bridges provide a way for games like Axie to support a large number of users on their dapp.

Originally, Axie Infinity was built with Ethereum in mind. However, as millions of users play, the game's designers had to build a layer 2 blockchain to accommodate the vast number of users.

When users need to move Ethereum assets on or off of the Axie game, they use the Ronin bridge. This bridge is used to wrap ether tokens into wETH that are used in the game. Axie tokens are named Smooth Love Potion or SLP. Since SLP is a game-only token, it is not popular on major exchanges. Users need a way to cash in and cash out of SLP to get something tradable on the crypto market. When users wanted to cash out, they would unwrap those tokens using the bridge.

Bridges and Security

There is a downside to bridges: they pose a security issue by bringing another level of complexity to transactions and chains. As a result, the Ronin bridge in 2022 was compromised. The hacker found a security flaw and stole $650 million worth of cryptocurrency.

The developers behind Axie have worked on restoring user funds and on a new version of Ronin. However, the crux of the matter is that "cross-chain" technology is susceptible to attack. In fact, it is susceptible to both human error and "social engineering". Social engineering is the act of gaining the trust of an unsuspecting person. This trust is used to gain access to sensitive information like account log-in or bank details. Whenever interacting in the world of crypto, one needs to be aware of these inherent risks.

Exciting areas like gaming are capturing the attention of a new group of users. Games like Axie are complex. They need the player to use a bridge and in-browser wallets, but the incentive to earn in-game crypto is enticing to users. The reward exceeds the pain of getting set up. Web3 has the capability to offer new types of software for people, and Axie is a great example of this. There will someday be a huge amount of these types of games to play. Yet, there's still some risk. Crypto volatility also remains an issue. These are impediments, but there is growing demand.

In the End

Today, there is a lot of money in the DeFi and web3 ecosystem. Billions of dollars are being exchanged throughout the world, and yet, it is only a small part of a larger ecosystem.

Web3 and DeFi have a lot of components. There is a lot of ground to cover in trying to understand them. They are an evolution of the Bitcoin whitepaper and the Ethereum platform. This has resulted from the ability of developers to build software on top of blockchains. There's a lot of exciting experimentation going on. With experimentation, there is a great degree of risk and potential reward. It's always wise to stick with the idea... never spend more than you can afford to lose!

And yet, user demand is pushing developers to devise economics for these systems to work. One of these novel innovations is the idea of non-fungible tokens, NFTs.

Things to Know From This Chapter:

- Decentralized applications (dapps) are smart contract-based software that operates outside of centralized systems and provide more possibilities

- Decentralized finance (DeFi) is used and helpful to those with no banking access, those who distrust banks and those who want to bypass traditional banking regulation

- A DEX or decentralized exchanges are smart contract-powered crypto exchanges with no middlemen

- DeFi and dapps in general are not regulated, it's distributed and decentralized which is can be beneficial but can also be considered like the "wild west"

Chapter Eight

NFTs

B lockchains enable permanent records of information. It's one of the ingenious ideas laid out in the bitcoin whitepaper, and it is used across most cryptocurrencies. With blockchain, ownership, time, and other specific data can be "stamped," which is turned into a permanent record, creating a new type of ownership in the digital realm. This is what non-fungible tokens, or NFTs, enable.

Monegraph

The idea of using blockchain for ownership started with cryptocurrencies themselves. The blockchain keeps a record of balances and ownership of cryptocurrencies across time. But it didn't take long for people to realize other use cases. One early project, known as Monegraph, founded in 2014 by Anil Dash, Chris Tse and Kevin McCoy, experimented with this concept.

Monegraph used a blockchain from a Bitcoin fork called Namecoin. It allowed for the recording of ownership of something - in Monegraph's case ownership of digital art. At the time, Monegraph's goal was to help artists claim ownership of art on the internet. A user of would sign in with

Twitter and choose the URL of something to claim ownership, usually an image.

Then, the user would pay a fee to submit a transaction to the Namecoin blockchain. This would create a recording of the verification on that chain. Many projects for verification like Monegraph existed from 2014 onward. This caused more people to explore applications for blockchain technology.

Provenance Blockchain Projects

Proof of Existence was another project looking at ownership on the blockchain. To do this, Proof of Existence uses cryptographic "proofs" and blockchain to verify code updates. Everledger, founded in 2015, uses blockchain to verify the provenance of diamonds. Diamonds are a commodity whose origin is often called into question since many diamond mining operations are controversial due to labor and violence issues.

Many of these projects provide verification on the blockchain, but they don't provide ownership. However, early efforts were beginning to come into place about ownership or digital recorded rights. Economist Hernando de Soto began writing about recording property rights with blockchain technology.

de Soto believed that blockchains could solve global property rights issues. He proposed that property ownership could help people escape poverty. These rights provide safety and security to those most in need. A company, de Soto Inc., was founded and funded to explore this idea in 2017.

Understanding Fungibility

By 2017, Ethereum had attracted many software developers. These programmers were working on smart contracts and Ethereum's ability to create tokens. The concept of "fungibility" was beginning to be explored. This was an extension of the idea of verification. Companies like Monegraph and Proof of Existence pioneered the concept of true ownership.

However, unlike the bitcoin and ether cryptocurrencies, this ownership was in the form of a "non-fungible" digital asset. Fungibility is a term that means the one-for-one exchange of an asset. It means the exchange is like for like. Cash, for example, is fungible as one dollar is worth one dollar - regardless of its individual serial number. There are over 50 billion notes for U.S. dollars in circulation. Most of them, unless tagged for some reason (like marked bills, as seen in movies), are "fungible." They can be used for any legal trade of goods and services and can be replaced like for like.

Non-fungible assets are unique—there is nothing else like it. Think of art. Original art is unique and one of a kind. This is likely why the Monegraph founders thought blockchain was well-suited for non-fungibility. Wine or classic cars are also examples of assets that are unique. There might be similar make, models, and years of a car, but each one has its own identification number, manufacturing time and date, as well as history—making it non-fungible.

Cryptocurrencies, as assets, follow this same concept. Most bitcoins, unless tagged or marked as used for nefarious reasons, are fungible, just like almost all other cryptocurrencies, That is, except for non-fungible tokens (NFTs).

NFTs and Ethereum

The first widespread usage of NFTs happened on Ethereum. Early projects included Rare Pepes, a collection of a variety of digital images based on a known frog character. Another was called Curio Cards. This collection of thirty artworks was created by seven different artists, with art pieces depicting things like high-tech apples and parodies of banks. In 2017, these NFTs used the main ERC-20 standard every developer was using to create tokens on Ethereum.

The most popular NFT project in 2017 was a project called CryptoKitties, developed by a startup called Dapper Labs. CryptoKitties are a collection of cartoon cats with various attributes. Each cat looks different; their features like fur color and eyes vary. Some attributes were considered "rare," and each cat had a "generation" based on its lineage.

The lineage part is important. CryptoKitties popularized the ability to create or "mint" new NFT assets, creating an ever-growing pool of assets in its system by "breeding" two cats together. This process created new NFTs that consisted of randomized attributes of each cat. The new NFT could have more rare attributes, which incentivized the breeding process. The rules of creation are random, making the minting process fun and exciting for CryptoKitties users.

CryptoKitties Clog up Ethereum

The number of CryptoKitties proliferated via breeding. As more people found out about the project, the market for CryptoKitties went up. Dapper Labs had created a CryptoKitties marketplace where people could use an in-browser wallet to buy, sell and breed kitties. In 2017, the Ethereum network was overwhelmed with ICO and CryptoKitties users, making it almost impossible to use the CrytpoKitties platform.

The clogging on Ethereum forced Dapper Labs to build its own blockchain called Flow designed for games and collectibles like CryptoKitties. In 2018, the Ethereum Foundation developed a specific NFT standard—ERC-721—creating a universal standard for NFT creators.

Older NFT projects created before 2018 that used the popular ERC-20 standard, for instance, Curio Cards, must be "wrapped" into this standard to be used. This is a similar concept to DeFi wrapping, where bitcoin and ether cryptocurrencies must go through this process. The ERC-721 standard helped fuel further development in the NFT space. For example, the auction marketplace OpenSea was founded around this time.

The Beeple Boom

A lot of this early infrastructure into NFTs eventually paid off. By 2021, the crypto market had experienced a prolonged bull run, and early investors started looking for new opportunities in the blockchain space. The pivotal moment for NFTs happened in March 2021. Visual artist Beeple, who started selling NFT art in 2020 during the pandemic crypto bull run, sold a piece of artwork for $69 million through Christie's auction house. The sale was record-breaking.

This event led to a furious amount of activity in the NFT space. Many creators saw the sale as a watershed moment that gave NFTs a lot of credibility. Bored Ape Yacht Club, also known as BAYC, launched in April 2021, with 10,000 different renditions of apathetic-looking ape art. This ushered in the fad of social media profile pic NFTs, also known as PFPs.

PFPs, sometimes just used, colloquially as "pfps" on social media, provide a way for NFT owners to display their property. Many Bored Apes owners would use their purchased NFT as a profile picture to show off ownership.

Another popular PFP project is called Cryptopunks. These are a variety of almost crude-looking artworks that portray punk-looking "degenerates" or degens. In some of the PFPs, the Cryptopunks are shown smoking, validating the degen cred. The concept of the degen is the idea of DeFi and NFT traders who work day and night like the 24/7 nature of cryptocurrencies, and they serve as artifacts of this new generation of digital art.

The NFT Gold Rush of 2021

2021 saw huge growth in NFTs. Twitter founder Jack Dorsey was able to sell a photo of his first Tweet for $2.9 million. The music artist Grimes sold a collection of art NFTs based on her work for $6 million. Grimes has said that the NFTs have been her most profitable project to date in her career. The woman behind the "Overly Attached Girlfriend" meme - a famous photo of an awkward-looking woman - made more than $400,000 with an NFT version of the meme.

Many other memes were sold for tens to hundreds of thousands of dollars. These NFTs were sold even though copies are still being distributed freely on the internet. As a result, a fervent JPEG gold rush emerged during this time, where people would find a photo already on the internet, and sell it as an NFT. Many did this regardless of trademark or ownership.

A complete collection of the 2017 Curio Cards project was sold at auction for $1.2 million in October 2021. In late 2021, a project known as "The Merge" sold 312,686 NFTs in a collection to 28,983 collectors for a total of $91.8 million. The NFT craze was likely a bubble. As crypto valuations have dropped in 2022, the valuations of all NFTs have cratered. The buyer of Jack Dorsey's first tweet attempted to sell the NFT, which is a great example of the market deflation. The 2022 auction bids were 99% lower than what he had paid for it, and the highest bid was around $10,000.

Staying Power of NFTs

What the NFT gold rush of 2021 managed to do was build a lasting ecosystem. While speculation fueled the demand, it doesn't mean there are no viable use cases for NFTs. One of the central hubs for non-fungible token activity, OpenSea, is still going strong, in spite of lowered valuations of NFTs.

OpenSea is a smart contract-based NFT marketplace. It espouses the open-source ethos of the blockchain world, and users must connect their own browser wallet to use the site. The platform currently supports multiple NFT-capable blockchains for marketplace participation. OpenSea is a place for price discovery, creation of new NFTs and auctions of existing ones. The creation of NFTs consists of a "mint," like when making tokens for DeFi. Many sales - which commence with what's called a "drop" - consist of a bundle of NFTs with a "floor price," the lowest price the seller is willing to accept.

The auction system on OpenSea is like interacting with any other smart contract. Users must pay gas fees to list an NFT and to conduct a sale, as they are both transactions on the blockchain. This requires a bit of know-how. Buying an NFT is basically the same process as any other cryptocurrency transaction from a self-custody wallet. Centralized ways of buying and selling NFTs also exist. These include SuperRare and Rarible, among others.

NFTs on Various Blockchains

Blockchains other than Ethereum and Solana are also supporting NFTs. Tezos, for example, is a popular blockchain for poets to sell their work. The Enjin blockchain focuses on gaming NFTs. These are digital items for players to buy and sell within games. The Avalanche network supports NFTs with its unique blockchain system. It allows nonfungible token holders to earn tokens on top of the protocol itself.

Two of the most popular blockchains for NFTs are Ethereum and Solana. Both networks have had capacity issues during times of high transactions, but they remain the main NFT blockchains because of OpenSea's popularity. Ethereum has in the past become clogged, and Solana has had problems with its blockchain needing to be stopped and restarted.

This is why centralized NFT marketplaces are popular, such as Nifty Gateway, SuperRare, and Rarible. All of these markets have a focus on different aspects. Nifty, for example, likes to focus on new collections. SuperRare curates an artist-type gallery of items. Rarible is a resource for on sports and collectibles NFTs.

NFT Use Cases

There are a wide array of use cases for NFTs, well beyond the original art scope as proposed by Monegraph back in 2014. Younger generations are adopting what is known as a "digital native" lifestyle. This is supported by personal computers, mobile phones and virtual or augmented reality. For this group, the concept of NFTs is something easily adopted.

Many are critical of the proliferation of NFTs, and that's fair. The outrageous prices paid for some NFTs may seem strange, but people have been collecting things for eons. Older generations are familiar with collecting coins, comic books and baseball cards. NFTs are simply a digital version of these collecting activities.

NFTs are no different than any other collectibles. All collectors know that some things become rare and valuable, while others become worthless. Blockchain-based collectibles, such as the NBA's Top Shot NFTs (which are clips of the best NBA moments), are a good example of traditional collectibles going digital. They exist to replace the nostalgic cardboard cutouts of sports cards in digital format.

There are licensing deals with some of the biggest sports leagues in the world. The NFL, MLB, F1 are all adopting NFT technology to attract new generations of fans who use their digital devices all the time.

New Frontiers for Art with NFTs

NFTs open up a new world of possibilities for those who like to collect. One example of this is called "generative" art. This is where an artist creates thousands of renditions out of one piece of art using randomizing software to create many different iterations of the NFT. Each one is unique to the buyer, and it is a great use case for the uniqueness of non-fungibility.

Enabling artists to better monetize their work is a key component of NFTs. The science fiction writer and early blockchain advocate Simon de la Rouviere, for example, uses NFTs to create visuals for his novels, a distinctive creation of his work for his readers.

Many science fiction writers have few options to publicize or monetize their work. They are often limited to specific journals or magazines in the genre. These writers are paid a few hundred dollars for publication, and it is hardly enough to support themselves. To foster sci-fi writers, de la Rouviere has started a company, Untitled Frontier. The company guides writers in the creation process of NFTs. For this work, Untitled Frontier does a 50/50 split with the creator, enforced via smart contract technology.

The transactions are split in real-time. This is another innovative feature of using blockchain technology for creators. Collaborators do not have to squabble about being paid properly and on time as smart contract technology automates and regulates this process. And collectors get unique items.

A New Web

What is most exciting about the combination of dapps, DeFi and NFTs is that the evolution of blockchain technology may foster a new model for internet users. On a higher level, the concept is often labeled "Web3." The reasoning for this name has to do with how the functionality of the web has iterated.

In the 1990s and early 2000s the internet was just known as the "web." It was a static place. The web was where things like newspapers could be turned into digital publications. The use of hyperlinks and search engines allowed users to discover new things, and publishing online required a high level of technical computer skills. One had to be fluent in a hypertext markup language, or HTML to create on this first version of the web.

The advent of "Web 2.0." occurred with the emergence of social media in the mid-2000s and 2010s. Creation and discovery became more evolved. Facebook, Twitter and blogging platforms led the way.

Apple mass-marketed digital audio devices in the form of the iPod. This brought on the popularity of podcasting and digital music, replacing the need to own physical media formats. Google's acquisition of YouTube in 2006 eventually led to a massive proliferation of user-created video content, with over 30,000 hours of content uploaded every hour by 2020.

Web3 Giving Control Back to the User

Many content creator tools are now owned by large, publicly traded corporations. Shareholder returns are the number one driver of these corporations. Companies like Amazon profess that the best way to serve the shareholder is via the customer. Yet, privacy issues remain a significant concern. These corporations use customer data to increase sales, which does not necessarily align with a user's best interest.

That being said, it is possible that creators will align well with the beliefs of the cryptocurrency community. Most early crypto-adopters were drawn in by an interest in open, transparent and low-cost platforms. Building services on top of cryptocurrencies, blockchain, dapps, DeFi and NFTs is essentially the concept of "web3." This revolves around creating a consumer-run internet, a web that cannot be centralized tech giants that are solely focused on profits. Web3 is really all about giving control back to the user.

Since the advent of bitcoin, it has taken a decade for this to begin to even come to fruition. Technologies are built one upon another, and open-source software has now allowed developers from around the world to build Web3.

The concept to remember is that blockchain technology is building a new internet where users have more control over the things they use. Companies are using data from people to make money. Shouldn't the people have more control over how it is used instead? That's the overarching concept behind Web3.

Composability

The open nature of crypto allows for "composability." This can allow these services to all interoperate together. One idea for composability is in the gaming genre.

Oftentimes, gamers will spend a ton of money in-game for clothing, weapons and "leveling-up" as their skills increase from playing a game. Yet oftentimes these valuable digital items are locked up inside of the game. The gamer usually does not have the ability to trade, sell or take this credit to any other game, and the value either depreciates or is completely lost.

Composability is a way to allow things like in-game items to be used across games and platforms. There may be some pushback from large game studios that want this value to remain on their platform. In theory, though, if enough users want it then these studios will have to concede.

It's possible to build new types of services boxed on existing categories—with new tools. Gaming, social media, messaging and content creation are some examples. Anything on the internet today can use blockchain tools to reinvent software. Cryptocurrencies, smart contracts, decentralized storage and identity can do this. That's where the "metaverse" concept comes in.

The Metaverse

The term Metaverse was first coined by the science fiction author Neal Stephenson in his seminal novel "Snow Crash." The metaverse is a virtual world that lives on the internet, and it uses virtual reality technology to make it seem real. In Stephenson's world of Snow Crash, the metaverse is a place of inhabitants, culture and saga.

Many have heard of the social network Facebook's transition to Meta - now the company's name. This is an effort for the company to get involved in the metaverse space. The company aims to adapt to Web3 and stay relevant in this new web3 iteration of the internet, which seeks to replace Web 2.0 giants.

Is the Metaverse a digital Utopia or will it be ruled by what many see as the evil warlord in Meta CEO Mark Zuckerberg? Is it the future, present or ideological fantasy? It's hard to say. But billions of users are on Meta's products every single day - the company owns Facebook, Instagram, Whatsapp and the Oculus virtual reality headsets. So Meta already has the eyeballs to put a metaverse project out that could become huge.

STEPN - An Example of Web3

Much of the metaverse is still in the realm of ideas at the moment. Yet there is some Web3 software available that can be used today. One example is the mobile app STEPN, built on the Solana blockchain, available on both Android and Apple devices.

STEPN is a game where users earn cryptocurrency for walking or running outside. Rules within the app prevent cheating. Users are required to walk outside, which is enforced by the phone's GPS. There is a set amount of "energy" in the game for walkers/runners to earn crypto every 24 hours. The walking for crypto is not dissimilar to a type of proof-of-work; it is overall a hugely more energy-efficient method than the electricity used for something like Bitcoin mining.

Before users can earn crypto for walking or running, with STEPN they must buy shoes. The shoes are actually NFTs, sold in STEPN's own centralized marketplace. The company behind STEPN receives a transaction fee for marketplace purchases and sales. The NFT shoes have different attributes depending on whether a user wants to run or walk. Shoes that are "rare" or have unique attributes have a higher value. The marketplace also offers special power-ups for the shoes, known as gems, to earn more crypto during walking/running.

Like CryptoKitties, STEPN shoe owners can mint new shoes from two existing NFT shoes. New shoes can have a varying level of different attributes per game's rules. The randomized features create unique shoes, and uniqueness, in turn, creates intrinsic value for the user.

STEPN Tokenonmics

Beginner users in the STEPN game earn Green Satoshi Token, abbreviated as GST. Users are able to swap tokens within the system from Solana to GST. There is another token in the game that occurs at higher levels—STEPN or GMT. Unlike GST, GMT has a fixed supply of 6 billion tokens.

GST in the early levels of the game is burned when users spend it. But GMT is expected to grow in value for higher-level players due to its fixed supply - the same economic incentive that entices bitcoin investors. Players aspire to get to higher levels in the game by walking or running every day.

STEPN gamifies physical activity using cryptocurrency as an incentive. It's an example of a new Web3 world where people can earn for doing simple mundane tasks. Some criticize the game mechanics of STEPN as they believe it benefits only early adopters. However, on the other hand, the app is helping people stay healthy by promoting walking or running.

STEPN is an example of early Web3 solutions. It uses crypto wallets, crypto swapping (DeFi), and shoes (NFTs) as well as utilizes a unique proof-of-work (GPS verification). The app is simple and straightforward for all users, no matter whether they had any prior experience with crypto, and it seems this is a way forward for users. The game simply pays them for their involvement, without requiring them to know the back-end is blockchain and crypto tech.

Does Web2 + Web3 = Web5?

It's still early in the advent of this Web3 concept. And yet, there aren't currently any particular requirements to classify something as Web3. Jack Dorsey, a co-founder of Twitter, is currently working on something called Web5. Dorsey is also the founder of the financial services company Block, (formerly Square), which has been experimenting with blockchain technology since 2014.

Block has a lot of experience in the payments space. Dorsey sees cryptocurrencies as well suited for creating a global digital-only money system. He particularly thinks bitcoin is well-suited for this vision. It makes sense, then, that the company mines bitcoin and utilizes a BTC payments system called Lightning Network for small transactions. In addition, Dorsey's Block operates a brokerage service via its Cash mobile app that allows its users to buy bitcoin.

Some think Block's foray into Web5 is a troll on web3, calling it "Web2 + Web3," as Dorsey has been critical of the Web3 movement. He has said that it is funded by the same type of investors that allowed Web2 to proliferate

— the same people that turned their users into the product by monetizing data.

Diving More into Web5

The Web5 concept is based on Bitcoin, with no other cryptocurrency or token needed. Web5 is very identity-intensive— likely due to Dorsey's experience working in traditional payment systems. Identity is a concept Web3 is also working on. Being able to properly provide identity verification but also maintaining privacy using private keys is a delicate balance, but a problem worth solving in the crypto world.

Dorsey's Web5 core tenets are decentralized identifiers, verified credentials and decentralized web nodes. These are the foundations, from his perspective, for developers to build decentralized Web5 apps. In essence, Web5 is building upon the evolution of Ethereum - but without the use of open-source tokens; it relies solely on Bitcoin technology.

This is because many in the crypto world believe Bitcoin is the most secure and safe crypto system to build upon. The space for developers building apps on Bitcoin has been nascent before Web5. Time will tell if the concept of Web5 can bring Dorsey's vision to fruition, but it is promising that tech leaders are thinking deeply about this.

In the End

In a little over a decade, the crypto space has flourished from the Bitcoin whitepaper all the way to NFTs. Large companies are jumping on the bandwagon and want to profit from NFTs, Web3 and even Web5. The reality is that evolution and a revolution are happening on the internet powered by crypto and blockchains.

NFTs and Web3 are creating a more open and inclusive internet. An internet where artists can get paid for their work, and an internet where the user has more of a say in how their data is used. The key is to stay true to the vision and keep the power in the hands of the creators and users.

Things to Know From This Chapter:

- NFTs (non-fungible tokens) are blockchain verification of ownership of something - like art, music or other uniquely individual commodities

- Web3 is important to NFTs - they offer access to services on top of blockchain, including dapps and DeFi

- The Web3 concept is to ensure people have more control over how their data is used, and NFTs are often the gateway to ownership in this realm

- Some are critical of NFTs that it still prioritizes information being captured and controlled by the same organizations that turned users into the product by monetizing data

Chapter Nine

Other Cryptocurrencies

A s more and more people enter into the cryptocurrency ecosystem, new ideas are continually born. These ideas do not always align with the vision or the structure of existing blockchains. Because of this many new cryptocurrencies - in the thousands - have emerged, with entrepreneurs and software developers building innovative new blockchain concepts.

This chapter will cover many of the cryptocurrencies outside of Bitcoin and Ethereum that have been most impactful over the history of the ecosystem so far.

Litecoin

Software forks have been used quite often in cryptocurrency. Taken from the ethos of open-source software which is free and available for use in other applications, many developers have software "forked" or copied bitcoin's code and used it for other purposes. One of the most well-known projects in this vein is the Litecoin software fork. This cryptocurrency was founded in 2011 by Charlie Lee, who was a software developer at Google at the time.

Lee, a big believer in precious metals like gold, concluded the cryptocurrency ecosystem could use a "silver to Bitcoin's gold." He considered Bitcoin to be like a digital form of gold. This was due to Bitcoin's limited supply, value, and mining attributes. Lee believed that the cryptocurrency market needed multiple precious assets.

Lee had seen many Bitcoin software forks that had launched using a method called "premined." In premining, the founders mine the cryptocurrency to keep for themselves, before launching it to the public. Most founders were anonymous, which allowed them to collect a part of the circulation before anyone else. Lee wanted to launch a cryptocurrency more equitably to the crypto community.

Litecoin's More Fair Launch

Charlie Lee thought premining was bad taste and unethical. He felt this practice could be likened to a 'pump and dump' scheme. A pump and dump scheme is the illegal practice of increasing an asset value through false, misleading or greatly exaggerated statements. The originator pumps up the price to significantly increase it and then sells or 'dump' their position, and the hype around the asset dies down.

Lee set out to launch a cryptocurrency that would grow based on increased usefulness, and not just hype. In October 2011, Lee announced the Litecoin network on a popular messaging board. It would have 2.5-minute block times versus Bitcoin's 10 minutes and use a different proof-of-work mining algorithm from Bitcoin called Scrypt. While Bitcoin's SHA-256 requires computer power to run, Scrypt requires memory in an attempt to attract hobbyists instead of larger-scale mining operations.

These features were in response to Bitcoin's slow transaction times and the decline of hobbyist miners. Today, Litecoin is in the top 25 coin market capitalization. Its primary use case was to have faster block times to help make expedient payments on the blockchain. Unfortunately, a decade after its launch, its use as a payment mechanism has not yet come to fruition. However, because of its recognition in the crypto community, it is often used as a testing ground of sorts for new features that aren't yet implemented on Bitcoin.

Primecoin and Mining with Purpose

Another early Bitcoin software fork was Primecoin, launched in 2013 by Sunny King, who had started another Bitcoin software fork previously called Peercoin. Primecoin attempted to address the issue of cryptocurrency miners solving "worthless" proof-of-work equations. It garnered many fans among early cryptocurrency advocates.

Bitcoin and other cryptocurrencies are mined using algorithms that solve arbitrary mathematical problems. This means the "answers" to these "problems" have no value outside of mining itself. Primecoin set out to develop a mining system that produced an output that had value outside of cryptocurrency. In the case of Primecoin, the algorithm would solve for prime numbers. These results would then be published on a public blockchain ledger. The output would be available for use by scientists, mathematicians and the general public.

Primecoin proved that proof-of-work mining could be used to produce something of value other than just cryptocurrency and its requisite transactions. It maintained the core tenets of proof-of-work: Solves difficult problems, easy to verify and difficulty can be adjusted. In spite of its practical applications, as solving prime numbers is important in mathematics, Primecoin has failed to gain any mainstream traction.

Litecoin and Primecoin were important and well-thought-out early bitcoin forks. Yet perhaps the most well-known that has sparked mainstream interest in crypto is Dogecoin. Unknowingly, it became the first "meme coin".

Dogecoin and the Invention of Meme Coins

A meme coin is a cryptocurrency that originates from an internet meme or is otherwise considered humorous. It may be even used as a critique of the cryptocurrency market. The term is often dismissive, but some have reached high market capitalizations and some usage despite their ironic nature. The most famous meme coin is Dogecoin. Started by product designer Jackson Palmer and programmer Billy Markus, Dogecoin was created as a joke.

The pair decided to create a Bitcoin fork after a couple of beers, and they made the popular Shiba Inu dog meme the face of Dogecoin. The circulation cap of the coin was left open, and block times were reduced to mere seconds. Like Litecoin, the network used Scrypt mining to reward hobbyists versus profit-seekers. The block reward for mining was set at 10,000 dogecoin (DOGE) per block.

Neither Palmer nor Markus realized early on that they had created the first meme coin, one of many to come. Bitcoin used mailing lists and cryptographic message boards to gain users over time, while Dogecoin turned to social media to amass a large user base. Palmer took to Twitter, and on

November 28, 2013, he tweeted, "Investing in Dogecoin, pretty sure it's the next big thing." And indeed, Palmer spoke it into existence. Dogecoin took off, with friendly memes and a low price. In 2013, Dogecoin was worth fractions of a cent. Little did the founders know that later on, during a global pandemic, its price would grow by multiples.

It's important to keep in mind meme coins can rise and fall in price quickly, and might not be a great store of value when compared to other cryptocurrencies.

Evolution of Mining

With the introduction of new coins came new methods of mining. Scrypt mining is used in both Litecoin and Dogecoin. In time, hardware designers found a way to use Scrypt to create mining machines for the coins. Since Scrypt requires the storage of large amounts of numbers, the temporary Random Access Memory (RAM) chip needed to be very powerful.

Hardware designers were able to create chips to do this, which are known as Application-Specific Instruction Circuits, or ASICs. Once again, this took the hobbyist out of supporting the network. Profit reigns as king when it comes to crypto mining, and it seems no coin, regardless of the founder's intentions, can avoid that fate.

For this and other reasons, early cryptocurrency enthusiasts around 2013 started thinking about a new type of mining process. They set out to upend the incumbent proof-of-work, and the most popular alternative became something called "proof-of-stake" or PoS. The idea behind PoS is to utilize crypto holder's balances to "stake" the network to provide security, because any attack by these stakers would result in these balances being wiped out.

Early Proof-of-Stake Cryptocurrencies

The first coin to use proof-of-stake for mining was a bitcoin software fork called Peercoin, which was invented by Sunny King, also the founder of Primecoin, as mentioned above. Holders were able to "stake" peercoins to provide support for the network. In return for this staking, these holders would be able to mint new coins.

The PoS model is not without its flaws. One is that as a result of this process, the "rich get richer" because only those who actually have coins can generate new ones. This is unlike in bitcoin hobbyist mining where anyone with a computer could jump onto the cryptocurrency train.

Nevertheless, several projects began adopting PoS as an alternative to proof-of-work.

This includes the anonymous NXT project and Bitshares. Bitshares' controversial founder Dan Larimer would be later involved in several other blockchains, including the social media-centric Steemit and Ethereum rival EOS. The proof-of-stake model has become an efficient model for other cryptocurrencies. The Ethereum network has adopted this in an ambitious upgrade in 2022.

Token Standards

Token standards allow software developers to create different types of cryptocurrencies within the Ethereum ecosystem. These cryptocurrencies have their own blockchains and can be used for different applications, with the most popular among them being the ERC-20 tokens. These coins are similar in use to ether tokens but can be deployed for different networks.

The Ethereum platform introduced the concept of token standards. Before this, standardization did not exist in cryptocurrency. To launch a new cryptocurrency, projects had to copy Bitcoin, which had limited functionality. Alternatively, they could create a completely new protocol, which is no small task. Ethereum has a set of standards known as ERC, which stands for "Ethereum request for comment." It is a similar concept devised by a group called the Internet Engineering Task Force. These standards serve to convey essential technical notes and requirements to a group of software developers.

The concept of token standards introduced "composability" to cryptocurrency. Composability means every coin created on Ethereum could interact with others, which would become important when decentralized exchanges gained traction. The Ethereum standard allowed any token to be traded on these types of platforms.

A few other Ethereum token standards to note include ERC-721. This is the standard for non-fungible tokens, or NFTs. Two other important standards are ERC-777 and ERC-1155; the former provides extra functionality for privacy and recovery, while the latter is more efficient as it bundles transactions together for cost savings.

Ethereum Competitors

Efficiency and cost savings are important on the Ethereum platform. As ether spikes in popularity, so has the price of transactions, making it difficult to use. It meant slow transaction times and high gas fees on the network during periods of high use, which some refer to as congestion.

Competing smart contract platforms have come along to rival Ethereum. While Ethereum has a lot of traction with software engineers today, that doesn't mean another platform can't come along and upend it if it offers a superior product. The majority of software developers discover Bitcoin, then Ethereum. And while many learn how to use smart contracts via Ethereum, many are moving to other blockchains.

Ethereum has some technical constraints, which the Ethereum Foundation does work hard to remove. However, there are a number of blockchains that have been created with the tenets of Ethereum in mind with new features. Speed, security and usability are a few of the reasons why these alternatives, sometimes called Ethereum Killers, exist.

Avalanche

Competing smart contract platforms are available today, such as Avalanche or (AVA). It was developed by a group of Cornell University computer scientists that saw inefficiencies with Ethereum early on. Some of these flaws include the number of transactions per second, security and the ability for the network to grow to millions of users. Avalanche improved upon those flaws, building a new blockchain from the ground up.

The project says it is energy efficient and can scale up to many users by providing a more evenly distributed network. Avalanche can process 4,500 transactions per second with a technology called Direct A. It also uses several different blockchains in its network in order to reduce blockchain bottlenecks that could limit the number of users. Software developers can build "subnets" on Avalanche, creating their own blockchain networks, cryptocurrencies and rules.

Avalanche (AVAX) is the cryptocurrency used on the blockchain. The Avalanche network uses a proof-of-stake system. Participants who stake are known as "validators," and this requires them to put up a small stake of

2,000 AVA to support the network. However, the incentives are different from most proof-of-stake networks. Fees on Avalanche are "burned" or destroyed in the system. The system has its own method of exchange known as the X-Chain, allowing users to exchange them among themselves.

Solana

Another noteworthy Ethereum competitor is Solana (SOL). Solana claims to be faster, providing more than 710,000 transactions per second for around a $0.00025 fee for each one. Solana is able to do this by implementing a few new concepts to its blockchain network. Solana uses proof-of-stake, avoiding miners that expect rewards for supporting the network. It also uses proof-of-history (POH) so that transactions can be ordered as they come rather than by blocks at an interval of time. These might prove to take too long for the transactions to be processed. PoH is used as a performance improvement, not a consensus method like proof-of-stake.

Many also believe Solana is a lot more centralized than Ethereum, but this may be a more ideological facet of the network rather than a technical one. In theory, centralized blockchains might perform better than decentralized ones over time. Solana has token standards, and the most known is the SPL standard (Solana program library).

Some of the criticisms of Solana have proved true, as it was revealed that the disgraced FTX crypto exchange founder Sam Bankman-Fried was a big financial influence on the network. The Solana community has downplayed this. Also concerning is that Solana has experienced several outages in its history, requiring restarts of the blockchain. When Solana goes down, any dapp running on the network can't process transactions, which renders a decentralized application useless until it is running again.

Binance Smart Chain

Binance Smart Chain, or BSC, is another competitor to Ethereum. BSC uses a "dual chain" system employing two blockchains to help the network with efficiency. One blockchain is for simple transactions. The other chain is for interacting with smart contracts so that the network doesn't get clogged with smart contract transactions. This allows simple payment transactions to maintain their network speed.

BSC has devised its own type of proof-of-stake called proof-of-stake authority, or PoSA. In this system, holders of the native token (Binance Coin or BNB) stake their holdings. In return, these holders are "validators" and get more BNB in return for supporting the network. There is no supply of new tokens with BSC, unlike Bitcoin for example, which has a fixed number of bitcoins which continue to be mined.

The cryptocurrency exchange Binance controls the supply, and it will often "burn" or remove tokens from the network. Binance Smart Chain, like Ethereum, has different token types. For example, BEP-20 is the same type of standard as Ethereum's ERC-20 tokens. BSC is considered controversial as its parent company Binance has been under a lot of scrutiny by regulators around the world for dishonest and potentially illegal business practices.

EOS

EOS (EOS) is another Ethereum competitor. Many people know it for raising a blockbuster $4.1 billion ICO in 2018 to raise funds to launch the network. To build something fast, EOS uses something called parallel processing, allowing the network to break down information into parts. The PoS network utilizes "block producers" that own computing power with their staking to run fast transactions. The block producers are able to set their own fees on the network since they own the computing power.

EOS set out to create a business-focused platform for developers and block producers. Many open source blockchains are not attractive to businesses. This is because there are specific requirements businesses need, including reliability, security and the ability to identify users for compliance purposes.

There have been centralization concerns with EOS as some users are worried that the EOS Foundation maintains too much platform control. The purpose of blockchain is to use technology to remove centralized governance, but antagonists believe block producers have incentive to control large parts of the network. Ultimately, if block producers hold too much power, it is no different than any other centralized platform or company.

WAX

Worldwide Asset Exchange, or WAX, is another Ethereum rival that launched in 2017. It uses delegated proof of stake (DPoS), in which mining is conducted via holding coins, and as the name suggests, voting rights can be "delegated." This is similar to how congressmen have constituents. The WAX delegation allows for voting and governance on the network.

The WAX network has long supported the gaming industry. In fact, it was launched to help to decentralize games. Currently, the gaming industry is owned by a small number of large corporations that control the development of new games and limit users' ability to monetize "in-game assets".

Many gamers collect these in-game assets while playing. These can include a player's clothing, weapons or special power-ups. But oftentimes in games, these assets are locked inside a centralized system owned by a gaming company for their own profit. WAX's primary features include the ability to launch a token within a gaming ecosystem, allowing game designers and gamers to further monetize gaming efforts. Essentially by opening these desired game tokens for purchase by the consumers or gamers.

Emerging Smart Contract Blockchains

The networks mentioned above currently support decentralized applications in some form. And these are just examples. Emerging smart contract blockchains also include NEAR and Hive, among many others. In addition, there are other networks in a long process of deploying smart contract capabilities.

These include Cardano, founded by Ethereum co-founder Charles Hoskinson. Also Polkadot, started by early Ethereum co-founder Gavin Wood. Nevertheless, the Ethereum blockchain continues to be the leader in smart contracts. It is racing ahead to provide next-generation tools and is constantly working on upgrades.

Meanwhile, competitors are continuing to build alternative platforms with features. Software developers often get smart contract experience from studying Ethereum and how it works. But today there are an increasing number of blockchains to work on. This helps the ecosystem to better diversify, and investors have chances to deploy capital on the chains they think might scale to millions or billions of users, which they expect cryptocurrency prices to appreciate on the chains that eventually win.

Layer 2 Networks

Because of the lack of speed that exists on some blockchains, the concept of "Layer 2" has gained traction. These Layer 2 systems are additional blockchains that can add more functionality to a system. Although not always the case some of these Layer 2 blockchains also have cryptocurrencies of their own.

Ethereum is the network that by far has the most Layer 2 cryptocurrencies. These include 0x, Polygon and Optimism, among others. Cosmos also has a few of these, including OmiseGo, THORChain and Secret. The Polkadot ecosystem has Kusama, which is one of the fastest growing software developer blockchains.

Each of these additional cryptocurrencies has their own specific technology and functionality to help "Layer 1" networks such as Ethereum, Cosmos and Polkadot. Technical constraints currently require these solutions in order for the blockchain and crypto world to properly grow and perhaps accommodate billions of users in the future. However, the crypto world is still in the nascent stages, and it is possible that in the future Layer 1 technologies may render some of these additional cryptocurrencies obsolete.

Ripple

Ripple is a real-time settlement system, currency exchange and remittance network. It was created by Ripple Labs Inc., a US-based technology company. Released in 2012, Ripple is built upon a distributed open-source protocol, with Ripple Labs being a for-profit company that steers the network's development.

Instead of mining, Ripple uses nodes that act similar to distributed computer servers to support the network and its native cryptocurrency, which is known as XRP. Ripple also supports tokens representing fiat currency, other cryptocurrencies, and commodities, as well as units of value, including frequent flier miles or mobile minutes. Ripple Labs was known for its partnership with MoneyGram to help facilitate cross-border payments, which are usually expensive using traditional methods (which anyone who has sent a wire transfer to another country knows well). The partnership ended in 2021.

Ripple seeks to enable "secure, instant, and nearly free global financial transactions of any size with no chargebacks" using its RippleNet and On-Demand Liquidity (ODL) technology. The ledger employs the native cryptocurrency known as XRP. In 2020, Ripple Labs was sued by the U.S. Securities and Exchange Commission (SEC) for selling its XRP tokens which the SEC has classified as unregistered securities.

Stellar

In 2014, Jed McCaleb, founder of Mt. Gox and co-founder of Ripple, launched the network system Stellar. He did this with former lawyer Joyce Kim. McCaleb formed a website called "Secret Bitcoin Project," seeking alpha testers. The non-profit Stellar Development Foundation was created in collaboration with Stripe CEO Patrick Collison. The project officially launched in July 2014, and Stellar received $3 million in seed funding from Stripe.

Stellar was released as a decentralized payment network. It is a protocol with a currency, stellar (XLM), and the network had 100 billion stellar at its launch. Twenty-five percent of those would be given to non-profits working on financial inclusion. Stripe received 2 percent, or 2 billion, of the initial stellar in return for its seed investment. The cryptocurrency, originally known as stellar, was later renamed Lumens or XLM.

In August 2014, Mercado Bitcoin announced it would be using the Stellar network. Mercado Bitcoin is the first Brazilian bitcoin exchange. By January 2015, Stellar had approximately 3 million registered user accounts, and its market cap was almost $15 million. The network is always adding new features through its Stellar Development Foundation. Some of these features include smart contracts, the ability to create tokens and NFTs in order to stay relevant in the continually evolving cryptocurrency ecosystem.

Storage Coins

Smart contract platforms need other technologies in order for them to work. The decentralized nature of blockchains means other parts of how centralized systems work are needed. For example, storage is one of the most sought-after technologies for smart contracts and dapps. Due to the distributed nature of cryptocurrency networks, many "storage coins" have emerged.

Storage coins allow developers to retain data in a way that prevents centralization. This form of storage is often called open-source cloud storage. Its goal is to upend existing business models deployed by tech giants like Amazon, Google and Microsoft that make money providing cloud storage solutions to businesses.

These large tech companies allow businesses to "rent" digital space so that businesses can store data without having to buy physical hardware. Centralized data storage has allowed thousands of businesses to start and scale, but open-source cryptocurrency platforms believe an even better platform can be built.

Storj & Sia

Storj (STORJ) is one of the earliest open-source cloud storage projects. Founded in 2014, the initial idea for Storj was to invent a new way to mine cryptocurrencies. Storj "farmers" use excess computing capacity to provide users with encrypted cloud storage. The project conducted an ICO, raising $30 million dollars.

Sia was another early storage project in the blockchain space. Founded in 2015, Sia (SC) decided to go with proof-of-work mining. Sia used the BLAKE2 cryptographic hash function so that bitcoin miners don't use the network. This required specialized mining equipment, which is known in the industry as ASICs.

This ASIC mining strategy for decentralized storage has worked for Sia. It now has a network capacity of over 2 petabytes, which is 2,256 terabytes - meaning that Sia can store lots of information in a decentralized fashion. There are hundreds of node operators securing the Sia network, and they host over 766 terabytes of files.

Filecoin & Arweave

One of the most highly-touted projects in the decentralized storage space is Filecoin. Launched in 2017, during the ICO craze, it raised $200 million. The project invented something called the Interplanetary File System, or IPFS. It is a totally distributed storage platform and uses FIL, the Filecoin token, to support governance in the project. Founded in 2014, Filecoin is similar to Storj and Sia but is in widespread use among the crypto community.

Another popular storage platform getting traction is Arweave. By differentiating itself from competitors as an archival solution, Arweave holds data permanence as paramount. The idea is to be able to permanently store data online, which has a subset of cryptocurrency enthusiasts excited about its future.

Many centralized storage providers don't offer any sort of permanent data storage. Arweave, with its own cryptocurrency, provides that to users along with independence from third-party brokers. In this way, Arweave is both decentralized and permanent, making it different from most data storage products available on the market today.

Privacy Coins

The next category of interest is privacy cryptocurrencies, which are favored by those suspicious of centralized authorities trying to stop cryptocurrencies. Blockchain technologies are not by themselves anonymous. They are only pseudonymous, and with enough data, it's not hard to figure out who exactly is controlling crypto transactions.

However, these cryptocurrencies are problematic with regulators, who see these are ways to circumvent things like sanctions. The situation is fluid for these types of assets, and regulators may decide to ban these based on policy.

One of the earliest projects focused on user privacy is Zcash. In 2013, Johns Hopkins professor Matthew Green and some of his graduate students began Zcash's development which would be later completed by the for-profit

Zcash Company under the leadership of Zooko Wilcox. The company raised over $3 million in venture capital to finish the project.

Zcash

The Zcash cryptocurrency provides enhanced privacy for its users. Zcash is based on the Bitcoin codebase and shares many similarities because it is a software fork, with one similarity to bitcoin having a fixed total supply of 21 million units. In October 2016, the first Zcash coin was mined. Initial demand was high, and within a week of its launch, coins were trading for a mind-boggling $5,000 apiece.

A trusted setup procedure was required to establish Zcash. This procedure would later be called "The Ceremony." It was vital that an enormous and truly random number be used as the private key and that no one person or computer retained a copy of said key. If a single person had access to the private key, they could counterfeit Zcash coins, which would destroy the Zcash system.

Zcash has two kinds of transactions, transparent and shielded. Transparent transactions are visible on the public blockchain, just like a BTC transaction on the Bitcoin blockchain. The shielded transactions go into privacy pools, which can be thought of as black holes where all transactions get mixed together. These pools ensure that no one can see where the coins come from or where they go.

Zcash and Regulators

Since its launch, Zcash has come under regulatory scrutiny. With its privacy features, Zcash offers users the option of "selective disclosure." This skirts anti-money laundering laws and potentially tax regulations.

The company has hosted virtual meetings with law enforcement agencies around the US to explain that the technology was not developed to facilitate illegal activity.

Over a two-day period, "The Ceremony" procedure took place to launch Zcash. The procedure was executed simultaneously in six different locations around the world. Each participant was unaware of who else would participate. Using this process, the private key was generated to initiate Zcash. It is said that the computers used to do this were then destroyed.

It has been learned that Edward Snowden, a famous NSA whistleblower and privacy advocate, was one of the six participants in the launch of Zcash. This should give a sense of who is involved in this project and the value some privacy advocates see in it. For the first four years, 10% of all coins mined were designated to the Zcash Company, its employees, the investors and the non-profit Zcash Foundation.

Dash

Another noteworthy privacy coin is Dash, denominated as DASH. It was originally launched in January 2014 as "Xcoin" by Evan Duffield as a software fork of Bitcoin. In its early days, it was subject to pump and dump speculation, later rebranding as Darkcoin and received press for its use in dark web markets, which are associated with illegal activity.

In March 2015, the cryptocurrency rebranded to Dash, the name derived from 'digital cash.' Dash was created to be the most user-friendly and scalable cryptocurrency. It was designed to protect the anonymity of its users while facilitating almost instant transactions. Dash's primary goal is to improve Bitcoin's transaction times and privacy issues. Additional features of Dash include Privatesend and Instasend. Privatesend allows the blockchain to lock in funds and make instant transactions. This mixes three users' transactions, making it extremely difficult to find out where a transaction originated, at least in theory.

Dash's InstantSend feature, on the other hand, allows a user to send payments instantly to another person. This means that if someone is making a payment at a merchant and uses InstantSend, this merchant will receive the payment right away. This is a perfect feature for a digital payment system as it resembles cash transactions.

Dash Master Nodes

Just like Bitcoin, Dash stores all transactions on a public blockchain. It does so to ensure users have enough funds in their wallets to make transactions. In contrast to Bitcoin, however, Dash runs a two-tier network. In the network miners and "master nodes" run in tandem, increasing the speed of the network and providing a more scalable network than Bitcoin.

Dash's master nodes take on some of the functions usually performed by miners. This allows miners to focus resources on securing the network, while also decentralizing the power miners might normally have. Master nodes essentially protect the network from rogue miners. Each master node must contribute and lock 1,000 DASH as insurance to the network, a type of staking. This ensures the master node operators' incentives are aligned with the network.

Master nodes are rewarded with a share of each new block. With these blocks come voting rights, which allow Dash to run as a decentralized network. The master nodes decide on the direction of the network, with each having a single vote on issues that affect the blockchain. The developers of Dash believe that this system of governance will help protect the cryptocurrency from being controlled by a single large group of miners or centralized third parties. Dash's network now has 4,100 master nodes, meaning Dash is a large peer-to-peer network.

Monero

Another noteworthy privacy coin is Monero, a cryptocurrency that uses a public distributed ledger with privacy-enhancing technologies. It conceals transactions to achieve anonymity and fungibility. Observers cannot decipher addresses using Monero, whether that be transaction amounts, address balances or transaction histories.

The Monero network is open-source and based on CryptoNote, a concept that was described in a 2013 whitepaper authored by Nicolas van Saberhagen. The cryptography community used the whitepaper to design Monero in 2014. Monero uses technology called ring signatures, and zero-knowledge proofs in order to remain private. These features are built into the network, and users can share view keys for third-party auditing if needed.

Transactions are validated through a miner network. It runs RandomX, a proof-of-work algorithm designed to be resistant to ASIC mining, which issues new coins to miners. Its privacy features have attracted cypherpunks and privacy-focused users. It is also increasingly used in illicit activities, such as money laundering, darknet markets, ransomware, and cryptojacking. The IRS has posted bounties for Monero tracing technologies. Monero is a return to the early days of cryptocurrency. While the technology and mission are progressive, the current use is nefarious. Only time will tell if Monero and privacy coins as whole can exist in a regulated environment.

In the End

Not all cryptocurrencies are equal. Many of them have different properties and offer varying technologies. Bitcoin's open-source nature made this all possible. The reality is this... there will be more cryptocurrencies in the future. There are already thousands, and many more are to come.

As people use cryptocurrencies, they find new ways to solve problems. There are limitless possibilities to what cryptocurrencies can do and how they will change the world. This is only the beginning.

Things to Know From This Chapter:

- Thousands of new and sometimes even innovative cryptocurrencies have emerged as the evolution of blockchain continues

- Many iterations of cryptocurrencies continue to arise, revealing strengths and weaknesses and varying degrees of regulatory involvement

- Dogecoin stands out in popularity even though it actually started as a joke and created the "memecoin" sector of the crypto world

- Software developers continue to learn, creating more cryptocurrencies for the ecosystem to better diversify

Chapter Ten

Analytics and Privacy

It may seem counterintuitive to talk about cash in a crypto-focused book. But in reality the original private currency is actually cash. When it comes to using cash, people have privacy by default. And despite the ever-increasing usage of electronic means of payment, cash is still there, and it's not going anywhere anytime soon.

Privacy is important. Especially in the digital world. The Cypherpunks were early advocates for crypto because they knew how important digital privacy would be. And could be.

Cash: The Original Privacy King

Using credit or debit cards or other forms of electronic payment always carry a big privacy risk. Electronic payments leave a data trail, including the location of payment, the amount paid and date of the transaction. In addition, those who control electronic payment methods are increasingly seeing this data as a source of profit. After all, large tech companies have already been freely using people's data to make money, selling it to advertisers and other data brokers. Banks, for example, offer debit card users incentives for certain purchases—a "trusted" financial institution analyzing your personal transactions for their profit.

Apple, for example, has moved into the payments space. Apple Pay maintains credit and debit card information; it even uses cryptography to secure and transmit data from users' phones to payment terminals. The company has also introduced credit cards and is now taking over the financing of its products, lending money to customers so that they can purchase Apple products. Other technology companies are doing this as well - reaping all the benefits of controlling the sales process.

This has its flaws. For instance, an ex-Amazon employee was able to use the company's cloud storage systems to hack Capital One's servers. The Amazon computers hosted customer information and the breach exposed that data of over 100 million users. The ex-employee sought to exploit this information for personal gain. It was one of the biggest breaches in the past decade, up there with the Equifax hack of 2017 (which was at a minimum a $700 million initial settlement). It's a sign that privacy isn't always guaranteed with credit or debit cards.

Eliminating cash would, in essence, remove the ability for many to conduct private transactions away from digital surveillance and potential theft. In essence, it would be a huge reduction in privacy if cash stopped existing. Fortunately, it's still there, with plenty in circulation. And although some businesses are attempting to go with electronic payments only, there are still plenty of people that see the value in cash.

Importance of Crypto Privacy

Cash is still legal tender, and a struggle to keep it that way could be on the horizon. Though some businesses see cash as dirty and expensive to account for, other businesses will gladly accept it. It's amazing to think about, but in the past twenty-five years, cash has gone from the standard payment method to a minority one.

While it may have lost some of its prominence, cash is still important. There are some who want to do away with cash. However, it serves an important function for many, and it has privacy features built right in. In some ways, cash has become a different tool than it has been for most of its existence. It's now a way to conduct private transactions in a world where electronic data collection and surveillance have become standard.

Unfortunately, through the decade cryptocurrencies have existed, its privacy has eroded. Whether by purpose or accidentally, as usage of blockchain technology grew, the ability to track transactions with high confidence has evolved. Much of blockchain tracking, also known as "analytics", has emerged due to regulatory and financial pressures. Early companies, particularly crypto exchanges, needed to find a way to track transactions related to illegal or nefarious activity.

This includes dark web markets transactions, crypto theft and offshore gambling. Since crypto exchanges wanted to be able to work with banks, crypto companies had to figure out where transactions coming into an exchange had originated. This was still important despite early crypto advocates who detested banks.

Analytics and Metadata

As a result of blockchain analytics, "clustering", a technology used in computer science to study data, was implemented for blockchains. Clustering allows the grouping of transactions and the study of blockchain information in order to track transactional patterns. Someone conducting clustering can, for example, study data about cryptocurrency addresses. This includes the addresses of various exchanges, wallets and smart contracts.

Blockchain transactional data is freely available. "Metadata", which is information that describes more detailed data, is crucial here. This is because clustering uses cryptocurrency address information along with metadata from wallets, exchanges and other sources to enable a clear picture of what's happening on the blockchain.

Those in the early days of crypto who were using bitcoin to buy things on illicit markets, such as Silk Road, probably had no idea crypto analytics could be used to track transactions. That's because the technology was so new that many assumed that bitcoin transactions offered anonymity and privacy. However, metadata has allowed blockchain analytics companies to tag addresses that interacted with Silk Road and determine the nature of their transactions.

Banks and Exchanges

As cryptocurrency and blockchain technology evolved and banks got involved, they required "know your customer" or KYC rules. Exchanges that wanted to have a banking relationship and offer government-issued money deposits and withdrawals were required to identify their users. Most exchanges require creating special blockchain addresses for each user when they deposit, making it really easy to track where it comes from.

Blockchain can actually provide a lot of identifying information in this way. The amounts sent, where they are sent to, and even the time and date of a transaction. The transparency of the blockchain actually could create open information like what banks already divulge about their users. Blockchain analytics firms are numerous, with companies like Chainalysis and Elliptic working with governments and law enforcement to track and prevent illicit activity on blockchains.

The transparency of blockchains has some trade-offs because of this. Despite the crypto ethos of eliminating middlemen or banking third parties, working with banks is a necessity. For the system to exist and function with liquidity, there have to be banks that do KYC and "anti-money laundering" or AML. As a result, many things are tracked on the blockchain.

Mark Cuban

Tracking on the blockchain is both a gift and a curse. Analytics has fostered an era where banks are much more comfortable with cryptocurrencies than they were before. Institutional, big-time money has entered the space as a result, thanks to the safety guardrails in the form of KYC and AML policies that are in place. This has led to more players, and more money, into the space. This is giving crypto more credence.

However, analytics aren't always good on public blockchains for privacy. Mark Cuban, an early internet investor turned billionaire and the owner of the NBA's Dallas Mavericks, accidentally revealed one of his Ethereum addresses. Cuban created a video NFT for the marketplace Rarible in 2021 and posted an Ethereum address there for buyers to send funds to for their purchases.

As a result, the address was tagged on the block explorer Etherscan. With a bit of analytics knowledge, anyone can take that information and track Cuban's portfolio to check out a portion of his holdings. And that's exactly what happened. Blockchain sleuths were curious to know what Cuban had in his portfolio. Some made fun of the quality (or lack of) of the tokens the billionaire owns, describing some of the cryptocurrencies in Cuban's portfolio as "shitcoins."

Public Blockchains

It should be understood that most cryptocurrencies and smart contract platforms are actually "public" blockchains. This includes many of everyone's favorites - Ethereum, Solana, Avalanche, Cosmos and many others. Actually, most of them that are in existence today are public blockchains designed this way for maximum transparency.

Most large companies in the blockchain space have a lot of data about users. It's not as detailed as what banks in traditional finance have about their customers, but it is still a lot. Addresses, transactions, balances, timestamps—all of that basic information is freely available since blockchains publicly publish that data.

Many people are starting to realize how transparent blockchains can be, and misconceptions about the technology are fading. As a result, there will be a growing demand for tools to allow for privacy. This is why one of the emerging sectors of blockchain is making public cryptocurrencies more private and adding more privacy features to the sector.

There are tools that can be used on public blockchains to obscure transactions, however. These are called "mixers" or "tumblers," and there are a variety of these services for different blockchains, with the most popular being, of course, Bitcoin.

Understanding Mixers and Tumblers

Mixing works like this: It pools many transactions so that funds are "mixed" with others in the process. These pools use long and often random periods of time in order to obscure transactions. In return for this service, mixers take a transaction fee from users. This makes individual tracking of funds very difficult, although it's still possible to determine whether a mixing service has been used.

Mixers aren't illegal today. While many crypto advocates use them for legitimate purposes like privacy, they are also used for nefarious purposes. When there are hacks and thefts in the crypto space, the absconded funds are often traced to mixers as the malicious actor tries to hide where the funds actually end up. Some anti-money laundering advocates say that mixers are similar to the method of "structuring" used to hide ill-gotten gains, often using cash.

Nevertheless, the lack of privacy on public blockchains means privacy-conscious individuals use these mixing services. One of the most popular for bitcoin is called CoinJoin. The service allows anyone to submit funds into its mixer, which is a big multi party transaction system. Users can send bitcoin to one address and get fresh bitcoin in the corresponding amount to another address, providing anonymity and privacy.

Tornado Cash and Tor

For smart contract public blockchains, Tornado Cash is the most popular mixer, globally. It supports Ethereum, Avalanche, Binance Smart Chain and a few others. It is a decentralized service, using a deployed smart contract to allow for the mixing of assets. Send some crypto to the contract, and get fresh crypto to another generated address.

Tornado Cash even provides a compliance tool that enables a cryptographic "proof" that can verify funds without detailing transactions. Unfortunately, Tornado Cash was banned in the US by the Treasury Department due to nefarious use on the platform. In 2022, a software developer, Alexy Pertev, began to face legal issues surrounding his work on Tornado Cash.

Other privacy tools in the public blockchain space include peer-to-peer mixing that doesn't use a third-party service. Instead, users work together person-to-person to mix funds. There are also privacy wallets that integrate with mixing services, for instance, the Wasabi wallet, which uses CoinJoin and Tor to anonymize bitcoin transactions.

Tor, developed by the U.S. Naval Research academy in the 1990s, is an internet anonymizer. It uses a technology known as "onion routing" to obscure an internet user's details like location. It was invented for military intelligence agencies to conduct their work. A commercialized open-source version is available for anyone to use. While it is not completely anonymous and untraceable, Tor improves internet privacy. The Tor Project is partially funded by the privacy advocate Electronic Frontier Foundation, also known as the EFF.

Monero

There are also more "private" blockchains, and they all offer different functionalities and degrees of usability and privacy. The cryptocurrency Monero is one of the earliest and most well-known private cryptocurrencies. Denominated as XMR, Monero uses something called "ring signatures" to ensure blockchain privacy when used.

A Monero user is provided with a set of public and private keys. There is a public view key and a public spend key, which are used to generate addresses to receive funds. A private view key is used to view encrypted transactions. The private spend key allows for signing the transaction. This is the process of using a public and private key in order to send cryptocurrency, as mentioned in earlier chapters.

The Monero network uses asymmetric encryption in order to shield transaction data. This is the same technology that allows for information sent over the internet to only be seen by the intended parties by using shared keys. That is why an extra set of keys is needed for Monero. Otherwise, users wouldn't be able to decrypt their own transactions. On the blockchain, transactions use a cryptographic digital signature that can be conducted by anyone who has access to the keys. This creates a "ring" of possible key signers, making it very hard to tell what one individual user is doing from the data published on the blockchain. Hence the term ring signatures.

Monero's privacy is often problematic for regulated exchanges that use traditional banking services. Exchanges are required to track crypto transactions as required by the banking industry. Because of Monero's privacy features, there are very few exchanges that offer it. However, it does offer good privacy for cryptocurrency enthusiasts.

Zcash

Another popular and well-known private cryptocurrency is called Zcash, denominated as ZEC. Zcash is a software fork borrowing from the Bitcoin codebase. It has similar characteristics to Bitcoin, such as the circulation of 21 million units. Zcash allows users to shield their transactions using something called zero-knowledge proofs, or zk-SNARKs. This is a cryptographic method to ensure proof of a transaction without having to reveal all of the details.

Zcash is well-known because a number of privacy advocates backed the project when it was launched in 2016. This includes Edward Snowden, the former government contractor and whistleblower. Snowden was revealed to have anonymously taken part in the key signing ceremony when the

Zcash network went live in 2016. A for-profit firm called the Electric Coin Company, or ECC, was backed by Silicon Valley venture capitalists in order to organize and launch the network.

Many exchanges list Zcash because unlike Monero, the use of ZEC's privacy features requires an extra step, known as "shielded transactions." In fact, the blockchain analytics firm Chainalysis has stated it is able to track 99% of Zcash transactions because most people don't use its shielded transactions feature.

Crypto exchanges don't support Zcash's shielded transactions. If a user wants to make an anonymous transaction, they need to move ZEC off of an exchange and into a special wallet that supports the functionality. Not all off-exchange wallets support Zcash's shielded address features; some only allow users to just hold ZEC.

Dash

After Monero and Zcash, Dash is probably the third-best known private cryptocurrency. Formerly named darkcoin, it rebranded because many associated it with the darknet. Dash has been around since 2014 as a software fork of Bitcoin. The community around Dash is one of the few Bitcoin software forks to have a Decentralized Autonomous Organization, or DAO, formed in 2017.

The purpose of Dash's DAO is to provide governance, as the network's mining structure is different from Bitcoin. Dash uses the X11 proof-of-work algorithm, and a set of DAO members support what is known as "masternodes" to provide transaction services on the network. The mining for the network is split between the miners, masternodes and the DAO.

One of the services the masternodes offer, in addition to a speedy transaction service, is the ability for Dash users to send transactions privately. The service is called "PrivateSend" and is done with a CoinJoin-type of mixing service, as Dash shares a lot of the same code as Bitcoin.

Horizen

Horizen is a company that builds privacy-enhancing technologies that can be used on blockchains. The network also has its own cryptocurrency that is known as ZEN. Similar to Zcash or DASH, ZEN enables users to utilize privacy-focused features right inside of its own network.

The ZEN cryptocurrency has "T-Addresses" - which is the name for its regular transaction addresses. In addition, it also has "Z-Addresses" - zero-knowledge addresses (allowing for increased privacy and confidentiality by obscuring the transaction information while still ensuring its validity), basically, private transactions. In addition to these privacy-protecting features, Horizen is also building a lot of tools for privacy-focused applications.

This includes the ability to use multiple blockchains via a privacy-enhanced "sidechain" called Zendoo. Sidechains are blockchains that are created for specialized purposes. They do not usually serve as main cryptocurrency chains. In this case, Zendoo is used as a complete privacy layer, whereas the main ZEN blockchain is public with shielding capabilities.

Secret

Started at the Massachusetts Institute of Technology (MIT) as a project called Enigma, the Secret network offers data storage privacy while being able to support millions of users' privacy. It started out as an ICO of the

Enigma (ENG) token in 2017. In 2020, the SEC fined the Enigma project $500,000 for selling illegal securities to investors. As a result, the project was rebranded as Secret, and investors were able to swap ENG tokens for SCRT, the new Secret token.

The project uses cryptographically-secure computation to run smart contracts. Secret is able to do this using the original research from the MIT Enigma project. By using something called multi-party computation (MPC) with specialized computer hardware, Secret is able to facilitate privacy within smart contracts. It is done by running the software on special computers that can provide "proof" of the execution of code without exposing the code itself.

The Secret network also supports private NFTs, which protect ownership data - the Mark Cuban issue as an example. Secret also enables private metadata, which is information attached to an NFT. It also has access control, which gives some leeway into who can view content as opposed to complete transparency which is the case of most NFTs.

The Secret network even has its own NFT marketplace, called Stashh. Unlike the blockchain and smart contract transparency inherent to NFT marketplaces like OpenSea, Stashh has privacy-supporting features. This includes private galleries, sealed auction bids and decoupling from wallets so prying eyes can't see other people's cryptocurrency balances.

Messaging

A number of messaging services are increasingly using cryptography and blockchain to make communications more secure. People generally don't realize how open some messaging services really are - the most glaring example of this is SMS, a basic text message available on mobile phones.

SMS actually stands for "Simple Messaging Service" and wasn't really designed for any degree of privacy. Some manufacturers like Apple use special text messaging software, like iMessage instead. However, iMessage isn't interoperable with other brands. So when an Apple user sends a message to another phone that isn't Apple, it could be using SMS, which doesn't have much privacy.

The usage of cryptography, messaging and cryptocurrency is likely to become more intertwined in the future. The transparent nature of blockchains necessitates a need for better-messaging systems. This is especially true with smart contract technologies like dapps, NFTs and web3 which is why it's important to explore some private messaging options.

Signal

One of the most popular secure messaging services available today is called Signal. With over 40 million users, it is available for both PC and mobile phone platforms, and has the ability to sync the two together across devices. The Signal Foundation is a non-profit organization funded by donors to promote privacy in messaging and development.

Signal uses cryptography in order to work. It uses a technology called "end-to-end encryption." This essentially means when a message is sent, it is encrypted using the Signal Protocol, and the message is thus unreadable to anyone until it reaches its destination.

A private key decrypts messages at the "end" when a user receives it. The communicators use these keys to unscramble the message. This way, surveillance of communications is made much harder with the use of cryptography—a feature in Signal that most other messaging applications don't offer.

Signal offers some other basic privacy features, like a notification when a user's "safety number" has changed. This lets a user know that someone they are communicating with has made a change to their communications device, for instance, they got a new device or changed their phone number. This reduces the risk of a malicious actor pretending to be someone they are not, often referred to as "phishing" or "social engineering."

Altermail

Another interesting privacy messaging project is called Altermail. It uses the Secret privacy network mentioned earlier to provide a decentralized email system. Email today is often not encrypted, even if users and administrators turn the encryption on. It's easy to transmit a message that ends up not being private for a variety of reasons, including sending to an email address that doesn't use proper encryption.

Altermail has created its own internal, end-to-end mailing system. In this way, people and organizations can ensure that private communications are secure from one end (the sender) to the other end of the message (the receiver). Altermail comes with the requisite address contacts list, file storage and other productivity tools most people use with email.

The biggest difference with Altermail is that, unlike most email and collaboration suites, the data needed to use it is not stored in some far-away server. Most email systems today, like Gmail, store email data on the company's servers. Rather, the Altermail system uses the Secret network's encryption tools to allow users and organizations to store their data themselves.

In the End

The amount of data everyone utilizes on the internet is immense. Large companies can use technology to analyze this data and people's behavior. This is true in traditional finance, and it's becoming more prevalent within the blockchain world. That was a key concern the Cypherpunks had with the rise of the internet—and a prognostication that has come to fruition.

There's a lot of work going on behind the scenes to make cryptocurrency and blockchain technology more usable. This is what's ahead and explored in the next chapter of this book.

Things to Know From This Chapter:

- Cash is actually still private and necessary - privacy is important on many levels and tools are being developed all the time to address this

- Companies get hacked and personal information on their customers is retrieved and usable for nefarious purposes

- "Mixers", "tumblers" and more privacy- oriented cryptocurrencies help to obscure public info on blockchains

- Banking requires KYC (know your customer) and AML (anti-money laundering) requirements, which can conflict with crypto-based privacy tools

Chapter Eleven

Tools

B efore entering the world of crypto, it's important to learn the tools of the trade. Crypto networks are standalone entities. They consist of systems for transactions and blockchain-based record-keeping. These protocols need tools to interact with them, and there are a LOT of tools out there.

Some crypto tools are quality, tried and true, while others are nothing more than hype. This is why it's essential to understand and know some fundamental tools. They are the way to interface with cryptocurrencies and blockchains, and this chapter is a guide to them.

Celebrities Get Robbed

The most important element of crypto tools is security. Security is never a fun word. Unfortunately, open blockchains lend themselves to fraudsters, scammers and hackers. Even Apple co-founder and nerd extraordinaire Steve Wozniak announced in 2018 he was bilked out of some bitcoin. Someone had purchased some bitcoin from the tech genius with a credit card, only to have that card be a stolen one that had the cash transaction reversed. Unfortunately, Wozniak had already sent the bitcoin to the scammer, and at that point there was no recourse.

This demonstrates the importance of security when it comes to crypto. The nature of cryptocurrency transactions is much different than, say, a credit card. With credit cards, transactions can be reversed or covered by credit issuers. By design, reversals are impossible in the world of crypto.

It's important to think about cryptocurrencies as a version of cash in digital form. Cash must be secured and properly handled. People keep cash safe in wallets, safes and banks. No one usually feels sorry for people who experience theft due to lack of proper precautions with cash. The same is true of cryptocurrency.

Hardware and Security

Security all starts with devices. The computer is a start— using high-quality computer equipment is important. The same goes for phones. It's better to not sacrifice high-quality electronics just because of cost. Platforms also matter, and this has less to do with brand names than what hackers like to target.

Apple computers and phones are, in general, more secure than Windows PCs or Google Android phones. Apple creates the hardware and verifies the software on its computers and phones, and Apple devices are known for a more rigorous security process than their competitors.

Their main competitors are primarily Microsoft computers and Android phones. There's nothing wrong with these products. However, it is important to know that hackers, viruses and malware are more prevalent on these platforms. When using any devices, make sure the software is always up to date. Running antivirus and anti-malware software is equally important.

Software and Security

Of course, software updates should be done on Apple products as well. But in general the risk of security problems are just lower with Apple products. Windows computers and Android phones take up 75% of their respective markets, and hackers prefer to target these devices because they can cast a wider net than when targeting Apple products.

Usually, viruses and malware end up on computers and phones via downloaded software. Never click on unknown or strange-looking web links. Don't trust unsolicited messages or emails with links to download content or anything. No matter how intriguing. Problems often start when something bad in the form of software is downloaded. The best place to download software is from the app stores. Whether that's the Windows Store, the Google Play Store, the Apple App Store, or the Google Chrome Store.

There have been reports of people being hacked or scammed via browser extensions, so always do research before installing one. Google them, and read the reviews first. Chrome is generally regarded as one of the best and most secure browsers. Even Microsoft's Edge browser uses its underlying technology. Chrome also updates itself as long as it is restarted often.

Two-factor Authentication

Whenever possible, opt for 2-factor authentication. This is a procedure that adds an extra layer (a 2nd "factor") of security on top of a username and password. Many passwords that people use have been compromised through data breaches, and scammers sell lists of usernames and passwords to hackers.

The website https://haveibeenpwned.com/ is a good resource to see if someone's password information has been breached. Password managers are another tool to avoid ending up on these lists - they help to store complex passwords. Password managers like 1Password and LastPass can help manage this information.

Two-factor authentication often requires a secure phone number. One way to do this is to make sure the wireless carrier connected to a cell phone has a PIN number to prevent unauthorized access. Hackers often call wireless carriers and use personal information that they have gathered on the web. They do this to switch a number over to themselves. This would render two-factor authentication useless, as the hacker would be able to reset your passwords.

This is why it's so important to ensure a wireless carrier account is secured with a PIN. It's also helpful to have another separate number, known as a Voice over Internet Protocol, or VoIP number. This can be used as a backup or even as the main two-factor authentication number. Mobile phone authentication apps, such as Google Authenticator or Authy, are also helpful.

Two-factor authentication takes security to another level. It requires another layer of authentication on top of using a username and password. This can take the form of a phone number or an authenticator app on a mobile phone. This requires action in the form of retrieving a code from another source to prove the person is real, and not a hacker.

Wallets

The very first steps for proper tools are to secure devices, software, and authentication. The next thing to look at is wallets. Crypto wallets store two of the most important pieces of crypto information, as this is where public and private keys are stored. But not all wallets are created equal, which is important to consider.

Wallets are generally categorized by temperature: Hot, warm and cold. The reason for this is related to key usage and the availability of funds.

-A "hot" wallet is one that is available at any given time. With a hot wallet, the user can conduct transactions at any time, just like pulling physical cash out of your wallet.

-A "warm" wallet requires added security to use. This usually comes in the form of multisignature or some other authenticate, so more steps or layers are needed to make any transaction.

-Finally, a "cold" wallet is used for long-term storage. This is the most secure form of crypto storage, and it often requires arduous steps to retrieve funds. When access is needed for these funds, they need to be transferred to warm or hot wallets.

A rule of thumb for managing crypto is that users only keep a small balance in hot wallets. Larger sums of crypto should be put into warm or cold wallets. Cold wallets are usually for long-term holding, often termed "hodling." Funny thing, the misspelling of "hodling" has turned into a popular meme from a long thread one user put on a message board eons ago.

Custody

The fundamental purpose of wallets is to securely hold the cryptographic keys. What's important to know is that many wallets don't allow users to control those keys. These are what's known as "custodial" wallets—a third party holds "custody" of keys for users. There are some positives and negatives to this approach.

For one, many users may not want to deal with the stress of controlling the cryptographic keys for their crypto. It's important to remember that these keys are like usernames and passwords. However, it can be catastrophic if they are lost. While a password can always be reset, private keys systems as designed today are not easily recovered and the risk is losing access to your crypto that no one can remedy.

Many in the crypto space like to use the saying "not your keys, not your coins." This is to say that with custodial wallets, user funds are at the behest of the wallet provider. Wallet providers are prone to technical mishaps, hacks and bankruptcy. Should any of these issues occur, user funds could be depleted or go missing.

Wallet Options

Coinbase offers different wallet products, and users can opt for managing keys themselves. While Coinbase offers custodial products that control users' keys for them, they also provide self-custody solutions. Coinbase Wallet is a user-controlled, non-custodial product, meaning users can access the private key.

There are other self-custody solutions available besides the Coinbase Wallet. The Edge wallet, for instance, is another non-custodial wallet that is available on both Android and Apple devices. Some people use self-custody wallets installed on their computers rather than a phone. For bitcoin, the Electrum wallet is a good option, while the Gnosis wallet is designed for Ethereum.

Many users like these because of the ability to store and control their own keys. Users also like these platforms because they offer multisignature security, offering an extra level of security. Basically, multisignature requires the "signing" of "multiple" keys for additional protection - this is why it's called multisignature. Some newer blockchains offer "client" software that has mulitsig built right in.

Seed Phrases

One way self-custody wallets allow users to safely store keys is by providing something called a "seed." This a series of phrases that correspond to unlocking a private key should it ever be lost. Any type of self-custody wallet will provide a seed for recovery. Users must ensure this information is protected and known only to them. It will allow users to recover a private key if lost. However, there is one downside to this - it can allow scammers and hackers to do the same thing if somehow the security phrase is discovered.

This is why it is important to store seed phrases somewhere safe. Always remember that hackers can perform something called "sweeping" if they know the public key and gain access to the private key. If the seed is not stored properly, the scammer can empty out a wallet before you even know it.

Again, two-factor authentication adds complexity to the security process. This extra layer of security is necessary when interacting with cryptocurrencies. When dealing with money, it's always better to be safe than sorry! And also again - it is strongly recommended to use a password manager. These extra steps will make anyone less of a target for hackers.

Cold Hardware Wallets

Another area of self-custody comes in the form of hardware wallets. These generally are "cold" wallets, used for long-term storage and safety. They are offline wallets that are hardware devices somewhat resembling computer flash hard drives in appearance. Oftentimes when crypto is shown in television shows or movies a hardware wallet is what they are using and looks just like a flash drive.

Hardware wallets are devices intended to store private keys offline. This technology has been around for a long time. Established companies in the hard wallet space are Ledger and KeepKey, and their products are known to be some of the safest.

It's essential to buy hard wallets only from a reputable vendor. This is because there have been cases where compromised devices have been sold, allowing wallet contents to be stolen. Don't look for second-hand devices or best deals, and always buy hard wallets directly from the manufacturer or the manufacturer's official store.

Other Wallet Functions

Non-custody wallets can do a lot more than their custody counterparts. For this reason, active users need to get comfortable with them. DeFi, dapps and NFTs often require non-custodial wallets. The primary in-browser "hot" wallet for Ethereum is MetaMask.

There are tons of different wallets out there for crypto. The distributed and global nature lends itself to many options. There are some subtle differences that users need to be aware of. Before making a decision, be clear on what kind of user you intend to be (active or long-term hodler), and check the custody offered, whether it matches your preference for a custodial or non-custodial solution. Also, the temperature of the wallet as previously discussed. Will the wallet be used for hot, warm or cold storage?

There are further ramifications of choosing a custodial solution. Coinbase, for example, has had to file with U.S. regulators. In the event of bankruptcy, custody users would become unsecured creditors. Custody users would have to use the legal system to recover funds left over from an insolvency. While Coinbase says that this is an unlikely scenario, it's possible. When dealing with crypto, it is imperative to always assess possible third-party risks.

Exchanges and Third-Party Risk

Third-party risk is a big issue when it comes to crypto exchanges. What is the third-party risk? This type of risk comes from financial institutions using outside parties to perform activities on behalf of customers - centralized crypto exchanges could be an example of this.

This means a platform outsources key parts of its core service to an outside provider. This can reduce costs and create internal efficiencies. However, it also reduces control and increases the risk for both a company and customers.

Centralized exchanges, which are the most popular, require third-party custody of wallets. Often this third-party risk is something that most users are not aware of. Decentralized exchanges (DEX) built on blockchain protocols like Ethereum require self-custody, which can add that additional security. A DEX is different from centralized exchanges in a few ways that will be explained in a bit.

Centralized Exchanges

The most user-friendly and efficient way to buy or sell cryptocurrency are centralized exchanges. Today, there are hundreds of centralized cryptocurrency exchanges globally. Each exchange is unique, uses proprietary technology and offers a unique offering of coins and are regulated by the country they are located in.

Since most exchanges are private, their financial records are not public, making it difficult to know the financial health of the company. Some of the concern knowing about a specific exchange company goes back to the history of the cryptocurrency markets. Many centralized exchanges have failed for various reasons. This has included hacking, incompetence or regulation.

Several examples of these failures, for different reasons, include Japan-based Mt. Gox. In 2014, it was the largest crypto exchange in the world, but it was revealed to be insolvent after 850,000 bitcoins had been stolen. Canada-based QuadrigaCX went bankrupt in 2019. The exchange had C$215.7 million in liabilities and about C$28 million in assets. China-based exchanges, including one of the biggest exchanges at the time—BTCChina, shut down because of the regulatory environment in China.

Like wallets, no two exchanges are made equal. It's often mind-boggling to decide what exchanges to use. There are some good rules of thumb to consider here to guide the way. It's generally better to use an exchange based on where it's located. The oldest and best-known exchanges, Coinbase, Gemini, Kraken and Bitstamp, are all based in the United States and Europe.

These exchanges also have banking relationships, so users can trade dollars or euros for crypto. Some exchanges, particularly outside of the U.S. and Europe, don't have good banking relationships and have to rely on stablecoins. With better exchanges, it may be easy to wire US dollars or Euros, or some other stable government currency. However, when it's harder to cash out, a reliance on stablecoins is used as a sign of less stability.

Decentralized Exchanges

Decentralized exchanges (DEXs) have less so-called "counterparty risk." This is a fancy way of saying that there are a lot of third-party risks (outside parties used to perform activities). This is because a DEX is powered by smart contract code instead of centralized systems that can often be opaque regarding the number of service providers and other third parties involved.

By nature, a DEX doesn't use any government-issued currencies at all. They all rely on stablecoins or cryptocurrency assets, many of which are usually volatile. And each different blockchain generally has one popular DEX that users use.

For example, on Ethereum, the popular DEX is Uniswap, on Solana it is Oraca and BNB Chain has Pancakeswap. There are even special exchanges for stablecoin trading-only, one of which is called Curve Finance. Trading cryptocurrencies on a DEX is also commonly known as "swapping". Swapping can often be done within dapps or web3, which makes it easy to convert into different cryptocurrencies.

Block Explorers

Blockchains are trackable, and users can confirm things like transactions, addresses and smart contracts with the use of "block explorers". This tool takes blockchain data and puts it on the web in a readable form. The irreversible nature of crypto lends itself to users needing these tools for confirmation and validation. It's important to send test transactions in small amounts before sending large values. Every blockchain has its own popular block explorer, and some of the more up-and-coming projects often host their own.

Bitcoin's Blockchain.com is the most popular block explorer for that chain. Etherscan is the popular Ethereum explorer that has capabilities to track smart contract-based apps, while the Solana project hosts its own block explorer at https://explorer.solana.com. There's also an independent block explorer called Solscan. Avalanche has its project-hosted https://explorer.avax.network/ as well as an independent SnowTrace explorer. The choice to use a block explorer basically comes down to user interfaces and features. Most block explorers are free.

Block explorers are pretty simple to use. All a user needs is a crypto address in the form of a public key. That key can be entered into a search box on the top of these explorers, and information will come up that is derived from the public blockchain. Since smart contracts also have public addresses, users can research these as well.

Sometimes, it's important to research addresses before sending transactions to them. There are a lot of scammers and hackers out there. One method the bad guys use is to claim an address is a smart contract or that a deposit address is fraudulent. Remember, crypto transactions aren't reversible— so use block explorers to research. They are easy to use and will often label reputable wallets, smart contracts, or exchanges.

It's important to keep in mind that not all crypto transactions happen on-chain. Many exchanges, for example, choose to run transactions off-chain for speed and efficiency purposes. Exchange transactions often involve crypto going into a large "hot" wallet. The transactions are then later recorded in a private database—obscuring the information.

Trading Tools

Most cryptocurrency users are obsessed with crypto prices. The term "bitcoin price" is one of the most popular search terms related to crypto. There are tons of tools to track, chart and analyze crypto. These tools track prices, market cap, total supply and other metrics users want to know.

Many crypto users like price apps like CryptoWatch or CoinGecko. CoinGecko has an extensive website available for researching coins, with information including protocol, ecosystem rank, and exchange location. They also have basic charts for historical prices and market caps. And all of this is free!

There are some paid offerings out there, such as Messari, CryptoCompare and Skew. But the majority of open blockchain information is available at no cost. There's nothing wrong with paid services, but they are often overpriced considering the data provided.

One product most pro traders do pay for is charting software like TradingView. This is also popular with publicly traded stocks. TradingView software lists different assets for traders, including commodities, stocks, government-issued currencies, and crypto. The most advanced features cost money, with a relatively low monthly fee. The service is available on the web and available on a mobile app for free with some basic features to try.

Crypto Media

Many well-known news sites offer free industry research. One of the oldest and most recognizable titles is CoinDesk. It was founded in 2013 (the author of this book has written hundreds of articles for this outlet). Other credentialed crypto news-specific outlets include The Block and Decrypt. Always get crypto news and coverage from reputable sources. Today, large financial news organizations like Fortune, Bloomberg, CNBC, and Forbes provide coverage of the ecosystem.

For crypto-specific news organizations, it's important to understand their business structure before trusting them. Some crypto news sites are not partial to covering the crypto market. Many of them are propaganda outlets that don't partake in serious journalism and provide readers with news that helps the business's agenda rather than the readers.

Be wary of news outlets that don't have a good editorial policy on their website. Check that the site provides information on who its reporters are, how or where they make their money and research their ownership structure to ensure there are no conflicts of interest.

Crypto Influencers

Misinformation in the crypto industry is quite prevalent. It's imperative for those entering the space to realize there is a lot of hype. This is often created by influencers who are promoting their own portfolios to people. These influencers are not registered investment advisors, and they may not even know what they are talking about.

The cryptocurrency industry is still very new. As a result, there are a lot of personalities on social media. Most are providing information without any real computer science, trading or cryptography experience. These people promote various cryptocurrencies without providing proper disclosure. In regulated securities, promoting securities without disclosing ownership is illegal, but this is not the case with cryptos at this time.

Be careful with the marketing and advertising that exists in the crypto space. Just because a project or token is advertising, that doesn't make it a good investment. Advertising will try to entice people to invest in the "next bitcoin," and these claims are often too good to be true.

The era of crypto marketing has proliferated in recent years. Turn on the television, and there will be crypto commercials. It's likely you will see your favorite sporting team is now sponsored by some new cryptocurrency. The ability to raise capital and buy advertising converts to value. This was especially true during the time FTX was popular before its collapse in November 2022 - there were many celebrities, who knew little about crypto, advocating for it.

Taxes & Reporting

Taxes are something many who get into crypto don't really consider, especially not until tax time. Fortunately, there are some tools available to make this easier for people. In most jurisdictions, cryptocurrency transactions are taxed via capital gains. Not all jurisdictions, so it's important to consult with a tax professional on these matters.

Nevertheless, it's helpful to have a tax tracking tool to keep proper accounting. Using a crypto tax accounting tool will help to report taxes. Many crypto exchanges will send out forms just like stock brokerages do. Using a tracker that can sync with various wallets and exchanges is still helpful. This will ensure everything is accounted for.

There are a lot of options for crypto tax tracking. One of the oldest and most used by longtime crypto users is called CoinTracking, but there is also CoinTracker, TaxBit and ZenLedger. Many of these products allow users to try them out for free before committing. Finding a service that works with your wallets and exchanges is essential. It's also key to finding a good accountant who can file taxes in the proper jurisdiction. Again, seek a professional for advice on this.

In the End

Every year, the tools people can use to access crypto and blockchain get better. But along with the development of better tools, hackers and scammers look for ways to bilk people out of money. Be careful, and always do your research. A lot of people have lost money in the crypto world by being hasty or not doing enough work on the security and research side.

Some of the information in this chapter can seem daunting. Crypto has a lot of opportunities ahead of it, and the tools are still maturing. But there are also many nefarious and self-serving people in the industry. This chapter may be the most important one in the entire book. And it's all worth it because crypto empowers people to free themselves and participate in this financial revolution.

But be careful. Use the proper tools available. Don't always trust third parties. Get past the hype. Leverage this technology properly and participate in the future of finance.

Things to Know From This Chapter:

- Security starts with hardware, always use quality brands - but security with software is also important, never download or click on unsolicited link

- Wallets for cryptocurrency are for securely holding cryptographic keys - whoever holds the wallet holds the security and ownership ("not your keys, not your coins")

- Self-custody with seed phrases protect and allowing recovery - non self-custody wallets have the ability to do more however compromises security by adding third-party risk

- It is always important to do thorough research to determine the viability of a crypto tool - use trusted products and avoid hype

Chapter Twelve

What's Next

S ince bitcoin came into existence in 2009, crypto has become a total new way to think about money. However, crypto can be extremely volatile and dangerous for investors. Does the volatility of cryptocurrency merit the promise of things like Web3? Only time will tell.

Is Crypto a New Stock Market?

People want to adopt financial services that aren't volatile. They want services that are not subject to prices that vary wildly. Today, using dapps is a novelty, and the price of cryptos fluctuates, whereas prices within centralized services like Apple or Google are stable. This is due to the use of government-issued currency.

It is hard to conceptualize volatile crypto assets as being a core component of Web3. People talk about the promise of Web3 (the vision and evolution of the internet from a centralized, read-only platform to a decentralized, programmable network) and the associated profits. They see the opportunity to make money on the price volatility. The problem is that none of this solves issues from a user's standpoint.

This is why stablecoins are so important. The rise of stablecoins has allowed emerging sectors in crypto like DeFi to flourish. If it weren't for the MakerDAO stablecoin being an early entrant into Ethereum, DeFi wouldn't be as popular as it is. Stablecoins allowed DeFi to take off, and help curb the volatile stock market-like effect some cryptocurrencies have, because, go figure, the majority of people would rather not lose money using financial apps.

Stablecoins and NFTs Can Enable Mass Adoption

Stability in cryptosystems is necessary in order for widespread adoption. Many innovations are happening in this area that will benefit users over time. Stablecoins and NFTs can help this. Stablecoins could help to better anchor the technology with users. Also, NFTs may be able to offer more innovation for digital ownership rights.

Today, crypto resembles an unregulated stock market. Yet underneath the hype and familiar platforms there is real innovation being developed. No one knows exactly where this movement is going. These new innovations are building blocks. It takes one breakthrough at a time before the floodgates open.

NFTs are likely at this precipice. There's been a lot of criticism out there about the utility of NFTs. But they represent the ability to own something unalterable on the internet. NFTs have given provable ownership rights to digital assets for the first time in history. That has meaning and importance as an anchor in the crypto world, right along with stablecoins.

NFT-Based Web Domains

Like real estate on the internet, web domains can be valuable due to their scarcity. There is only one "yahoo.com" on the internet. Ownership control of these domains is controlled by a centralized entity that can give and take away ownership. In reality, the domain platform is the landlord, and the domain user is only a renter.

Domain names service or DNS, the method of ownership control, is centralized. And this centralization has in the past been one of the biggest points of failure of the internet. In July 2021, a massive DNS outage caused AirBnb, FedEx and Slack to have service problems. This was due to one infrastructure company's problems with its DNS services.

A solution to this problem is to allow more control over domains. This can be done with NFT technology. As an example, for this book, the domain "blockchainbook.nft" was purchased by Unstoppable Domains, a service that provides domain names as NFTs.

"Blockchainbook.nft" has been minted as an NFT domain. It can be used to redirect to the website for this book. The name can also be a transaction address on Ethereum, and it can even host a website. This is done by using decentralized storage on the Filecoin Interplanetary File System.

Using Filecoin or other decentralized storage technology, things like websites can be online forever without a centralized service controlling the website's content. Ethereum Name Service, also known as ENS, is a similar service and offers domains ending with ".eth". This is why people often see the Twitter profiles of many crypto advocates containing these .eth ENS names.

Multisig Self-Custody

The concept of "self custody" is becoming more important. More and more people want to have the ability to control funds, usernames and even domains. And people can do this if they hold crypto private keys. There is of course some risk for anyone to store their own private keys. The risk of hacking or theft is heightened. But technologies are coming along to help mitigate those risks.

One of them, multi-signature (multisig) key storage, has been around for a while. This method requires more than one key to sign and conduct a transaction. For example, a company can have control of one key while one or more individuals have other keys, providing more security and distribution.

The most common configuration for multi-signature is 2-of-3, meaning two keys are required to sign transactions. However, there can be more complicated configurations of this. There are even multisig open source wallets available on the market like bitcoin's Electrum or Ethereum's Gnosis wallet, and they allow for complete self-custody.

Multiparty Computation

The innovations around self-custody are fascinating. One example is multiparty computation, also known as MPC. MPC has been around in the cryptography world since the 1980s. Even for multi-signature wallets, key storage relies on cold, warm, and hot wallets. MPC changes the way keys are stored so that status doesn't apply.

For example, hot wallets need keys at the ready, while cold wallets employ some longer-term process. MPC breaks apart the private key using cryptography, encrypting the information. Instead of having separate keys stored in separate places, MPC splits the key information apart. This information is put back together when needed for a transaction.

It does this by requiring parties to have hardware devices to split up the key, making it much harder for a hacker to compromise a single key. The key is broken apart, usually between three different parties using hardware devices. New cryptocurrency technologies like MPC are promising for furthering self-custody safety.

Cross-chain Movements

There is a growing need for the ability to move crypto assets across different chains. The idea of a "cross-chain" movement is growing, a paradigm that started with Ethereum. The ability to wrap cryptocurrencies like bitcoin and use them on Ethereum was a start. Now, the need has grown for various assets to be used across different chains.

Entities like centralized exchanges already struggle with this. Many of them support the Bitcoin and Ethereum networks. There is a hodgepodge of support for other blockchains and their associated tokens. There are two reasons for it: technical difficulties and security issues. Building out the transactional and security infrastructure for different blockchains simply takes time if done well.

Cosmos is an example of an ecosystem supported by many exchanges; Avalanche is another one. The main reason these two are often supported comes down to the fact that they offer support for additional tokens, which leads to increased composability.

Composability

So that cryptocurrencies can effectively interact with one another, composability is needed (the ability to interact and integrate with each other). In the Ethereum ecosystem, tokens, wrapped tokens and smart contracts all work together, making a vibrant DeFi and dapp world. In this way, any dapp using Ethereum smart contracts can interact with one another, like Uniswap contracts for trading within the dapp.

The bigger composability concept would be where dapps can interact between blockchains. For the most part, the tech is not quite there yet. Ethereum dapps and tokens only work on Ethereum. Solana dapps and tokens work on only Solana. Same for Avalanche - and so on and so forth.

Newcomers like Cosmos and Polkadot are building blockchains that interoperate. Cosmos does this by allowing dapps to run their own separate chain. Polkadot is heading in the same direction with something called Parachains.

DeFi Moving Chains For Composability

The internet is an interconnected network with different interoperable technologies, and blockchains and cryptocurrencies seem to be heading in the same direction. It's the only way that these systems can grow to a sizable user base without sacrificing usability. Blockchains, and by extension dapps, are slow when compared to traditional software applications, but speed will increase over time and usher in a larger user base.

Derivatives DeFi project dYdX is an example of a project that started on Ethereum, but has since moved over to building its own Cosmos chain in preparation for this future. dYdX gets many advantages by having its own chain. Cosmos allows dYdX to be interoperable with other chains. The company has built a software development kit, or SDK, allowing it to expand its ecosystem and not be limited to a single chain user base.

Polkadot, started by Ethereum co-founder Gavin Wood, is heading in the same direction. Polkadot is considered a "blockchain of blockchains," and it uses a framework for building cryptocurrencies and blockchains it calls Substrate. Polkadot can communicate across different systems.

Most blockchains are heading in the direction of composability so that they can interact with one another instead of being stand-alone networks .The motivating factors behind composability come from usability. Many early crypto adopters see blockchain as a unifier. A more adventurous world on the internet could be aided by the use of cryptocurrencies.

Metaverse Readiness

The rise of virtual reality (VR) and augmented reality (AR) will result in virtual worlds, and we are already seeing their slow emergence. These virtual worlds will be a place where people will look for escapism and special hardware will be needed to function. Virtual reality hardware in the form of headsets will allow users to play games and socialize virtually. Augmented reality, a mix of the virtual and real worlds, is also known as a stopgap. AR introduces some aspects of VR and all the while the technology continues to be perfected.

Cryptocurrency and blockchains are completely digital. Many foresee a future where they could be a major part of VR and AR, becoming a part of the Metaverse—a massive, open virtual world. In this world, people will interact with one another using cryptocurrencies. Of course, the metaverse resides mostly in the realm of ideas for now. VR has gained more mainstream adoption since 2014 due to the development of better hardware - particularly the Meta's Oculus - but it still remains in the early stages of its development.

Facebook renamed itself, Meta, to capitalize on the opportunity. It builds and manufactures the best VR hardware on the market in the form of the Oculus headset. And while no real AR hardware has gained popularity to date, it is rumored that Apple is working on a ski goggle-type AR/VR headset.

Big Companies Adopt Crypto

Ironically, it will take the efforts of large centralized companies to push the Metaverse concept to the masses because of the giant cost involved in developing VR and AR hardware. Can egalitarian blockchains co-exist in a gigantic corporation, profit-driven ecosystem? Undoubtedly, these two ideologies will be at odds.

Facebook, in particular, has actually tried getting into cryptocurrency once before. It launched the Libra project in 2019 to great fanfare after being in development for years. The idea was to build a blockchain for Facebook's various services, including the social network itself, Instagram, WhatsApp and likely Oculus VR.

The project pivoted to a stablecoin called Diem. It received push-back from U.S. lawmakers who feared it would circumvent tax laws and would have the potential for criminal activity. After many name changes, the project was sold and eventually deprecated by San Diego-based bank Silvergate Bank in 2022.

But Meta founder Mark Zukerberg still sees cryptocurrency as a salvo for his company. It has been said that Meta's efforts on the Metaverse are the CEO's number one focus. This is in light of their many privacy and data snafus over the past few years, which only highlights the concerns many have with privacy and large companies' misuse of it.

Proof-of-Work Versus Proof-of-Stake

The security of blockchain tech itself is also being rethought. Most major cryptocurrencies avoid proof-of-work mining because of the amount of energy use proof-of-work requires. The value of cryptocurrencies has created an arms race to build Bitcoin proof-of-work mining facilities as more computing power leads to more bitcoin due to the algorithm's design. However, this may lead to regulatory trouble.

Lawmakers are starting to realize exactly how energy-intensive bitcoin mining is. The entire bitcoin mining industry in Texas could power Houston—a city with a population of more than 2 million. Lawmakers are questioning whether this is the best use of energy.

There is a growing focus on proof-of-stake as an alternative, but proof-of-stake is not the only way forward for crypto. Some examples of crypto using alternatives to secure their blockchains include IOTA, which utilizes tangle, a proof-of-work that coordinates the network. IOTA is not issuing new units of crypto or charging fees; the network is user-supported. The platform is designed for internet-of-things (IoT) devices—small pieces of hardware like sensors hooked up to the internet. IoT devices are becoming a part of our daily life (smart home devices, wearable devices, etc.), and the data and their management is a growing concern.

Another alternative consensus mechanism is Ouroborous. It is the proof-of-stake system for the smart contract platform Cardano. Instead of staking, the network divides up transactions for processing. It installs a delay in confirming the previous few blocks to ensure they are secure. The idea here is to provide proof-of-stake capability with the security of proof-of-work.

The Flow blockchain is another example. Started by the team that built the Ethereum-based CryptoKitties, Flow breaks down transactions into smaller processes called Specialized Proofs of Confidential Knowledge, or SPoCKs. Anyone can join in and "validate" the network. It breaks down a crypto transaction into four parts: collection, execution, verification and consensus.

Storage and Organization

Chia uses proof-of-space and was heralded early on as an innovative new type of consensus mechanism, and it utilized unused computer memory to secure itself. Chia miners have scooped up tons of hard drives to provide storage for the network's consensus. Yet these new experiments are not without challenges. The rising concern is that it is wasting computer hardware or creating "e-waste."

Conversely, the concept of decentralized storage excites many cryptocurrency advocates. Filecoin, Arweave, and Sia are the ones that many find fascinating. They have the potential to upend the current models of storage. The idea of permanent storage is more than a novel idea. Hard disk drives need replacement over time, and decentralized storage could end this, so technical people are excited about the possibility.

This possibility also appeals to hardcore crypto advocates. These advocates see the potential for a distributed, censorship-resistant information system that would give data ownership back to the user. It sounds like the promise of bitcoin, a permanent store of value on the internet, or Ethereum, a permanent software system.

Ethereum Upgrade

As Ethereum matures, many other smart contract platforms are emerging to compete. Ethereum has gone through a very ambitious upgrade to its network in an attempt to keep up with the competition. The upgrade included something called "sharding," a way to distribute information across the network. Hopefully, this will be the answer to provide for more scale and a faster network for users.

There are two sides to the argument about Ethereum's penchant for upgrading. Many see the system's move to allow more transactions as a novel and well-thought-out plan for the future. Others see it as a cash grab since many people and projects already hold ETH. Whatever beliefs people hold, Ethereum is moving towards a continually evolving network.

At the heels of Ethereum are many other smart contract-based networks. Developers now have a ton of options to build distributed, blockchain-based software. In the greater software ecosystem, there are around 700 individual coding languages, and much like software languages, more variety creates more innovation in crypto ecosystems.

Ethereum Versus Other Smart Contract Chains

The Polkadot network uses "parachains" to allow various blockchains to interact with one another. On most cryptocurrency networks, blockchains are separated, running by themselves without any interoperability, making it difficult to move cryptocurrencies from one network to another. Many smart contract-based dapps are starting to run on a specialized blockchain, and interoperability is key to making these systems work.

Another example of this is Cosmos. Like Polkadot, it connects blockchains together, using a technology it calls the "Inter Blockchain Communication" protocol or IBC. In this way, the Cosmos network intends to proliferate an "Internet of Blockchains." Each chain in this system communicates with one another, which can be accomplished with the use of two types of chains: Hubs and Zones. It's like the hub and spokes of a bicycle wheel. Hubs connect the chains together and zones are where developers build apps.

Comparatively, newer networks like Avalanche and Cardano provide what's known as "modular" blockchain capabilities. And this all goes back to the lack of interoperability of many existing blockchains: A modular approach is needed for more users to come in and use crypto ecosystems. Think of it like traditional software like email. Email is able to interact with many different systems, creating one holistic network for communication. Blockchains are progressing towards this reality.

Scaling

Existing blockchains are racing towards this more modular future. Bitcoin is forging forward with Lightning, a long-gestating project. Bitcoin's main chain has limitations in the form of only seven transactions per second. Lightning uses something called payment channels, off-blockchain distributed systems that may allow bitcoin to be used as a payment.

The Lightning network is live but still not quite ready for mainstream use - but work is being done. Payments Titan Block (formerly known as Square) is a big supporter of this technology. It will likely be incorporated into Block's products, such as its popular Cash App, someday in the future.

Technologies like Lightning on Bitcoin—and Polygon for Ethereum—are known as "Layer 2," and they are pushing the progress of blockchains. Layer 2 and modular blockchains can treat the symptoms of blockchain's ailments. Blockchains often aren't as fast, cheap and usable as traditional financial systems. Companies like Visa have decades of experience designing payment systems. For now, it is difficult to compete with the incumbent giants but the tech is certainly improving and moving in that direction.

Government Stablecoins

Stable assets in the crypto ecosystem have grown. Governments have considered stable digital assets used in central banking, and the trackability of blockchains is an enticing technology for many countries for a variety of reasons. Some governments may want to have more visibility into their own money systems. These governments see blockchain as a way to progress a central bank's current technology. There's also the cost savings in digital currency over managing physical money.

Still, the idea of government-issued blockchain assets for public use is near. Central banks have been exploring this technology for some time already. The United States, China, and the EU are exploring it. Large payment companies currently have a stranglehold over digital systems, extracting fees from people and businesses. The hope with blockchain tech is to reduce those costs, and governments aren't going to ignore it.

Government Cryptography

Governments also aren't ignoring the future of cryptography. The underpinnings of a lot of this technology depend on it. The emergence of quantum computing looms large. In 2022 alone, the U.S.'s National Institute for Standards and Technology, or NIST, released four new encryption algorithms.

The purpose of these encryption algorithms is to protect government-based computers. Computer scientists believe quantum computing will break existing encryption algorithms if it hasn't already. Major military powers around the world have been advancing quantum computing, and it's definitely not something to ignore.

Much of the cryptocurrency and blockchain world was developed using governments and military technology, the same as the internet. It can be expected that breakthrough technologies will be incorporated into blockchain systems, making it more usable, private, and less expensive. The technology will be quickly commercialized to solve crypto ecosystem issues.

In the End

The ideological battle between centralization, decentralization and distribution rages on. Bitcoin is designed as a decentralized system. Yet, as exchanges, wallets, and other services cropped up, a more hybrid model evolved. The same happened with Ethereum and smart contracts. When Ethereum went live, there were very few tools to deploy smart contracts - now there are a ton.

The future of cryptocurrencies and blockchain seem promising. This technology can provide financial access, speed and novel new services. The combination of 7.7 billion smartphones around the world by 2027 means most people will have the tools they need for financial freedom in their hands. Cryptocurrency, blockchain, DeFi, Web3 and NFTs will be more accessible than ever by that time, and it's an exciting prospect.

You, by reading this book, are at the forefront of this new technological revolution. Welcome to the ride.

Things to Know From This Chapter:

- Crypto really is like a new stock market -but stablecoins and NFTs can enable mass adoption outside of just speculation

- Cross-chain movements allow for different blockchains to talk to each other providing more ecosystem capability

- Composability is where crypto can interact with each other and dapps can interact with blockchains

- Digital currencies have caught the eye of governments, to what end, is to be determined

All in All ...

In conclusion, the skepticism and criticisms surrounding cryptocurrency and blockchain are not unusual phenomena in the realm of emerging technologies. Historically, innovations such as automobiles, television, computers, and smartphones all faced initial dismissal and doubt before becoming indispensable in our daily lives.

The trajectory of cryptocurrency appears to be no different. As it continues to develop and integrate into various aspects of society, it is anticipated that crypto will evolve into a technology that everyone relies upon, often unconsciously, mirroring the adoption pattern of its predecessors.

Ultimately, everyone must determine for themselves how they will interact and pursue the use of cryptocurrency in their lives. Of course, it all starts with ... Understanding Crypto.

Also By Daniel Cawrey

Mastering Blockchain

Finance and technology pros will learn how a blockchain works as they explore the evolution and current state of the technology, including the functions cryptocurrencies and smart contracts. This book is for anyone evaluating whether to invest time in the cryptocurrency and blockchain industry. Delving in to understanding, way beyond just the buzzwords.